YOUR
SHEPHERD

20 $\frac{22}{2}$ 17

Cris,

May you catch a fresh
glimpse of the "Good Shepherd" in
the pages of this book. Evan
Conrois' story is on page 108
written by Cris.

TERRY KIRSCHMAN

God's Best... and Love
to you! Lin(da) Kirschman
Schmick

Heb. 6:10

YOUR SHEPHERD

Copyright © 2006 by Terry Kirschman

ISBN: 0-9770398-9-7

Published by

LIFEBRIDGE
BOOKS
P.O. BOX 49428
CHARLOTTE, NC 28277

Printed in the United States of America.

CONTENTS

INTRODUCTION

T*he Lord is my Shepherd!*" is more than an allegorical description from one Old Testament believer about his relationship with Jehovah God, creatively expressed in terms of his own experience as a shepherd. It is the Holy Spirit's prophetic revelation of Jesus Christ to every New Testament believer as well.

Psalm 23 has been the subject of countless books, sermons, devotionals, commentaries and artistic renderings. It is the best loved of all the Psalms because of the promises of blessing it provides to all who believe. And yet, to some, Psalm 23 may still be little more than a reassuring poetic passage of Scripture recited at a graveside or re-read in lonely, quiet moments of anxious thoughts or worried concerns.

This passage, however, is the divine revelation of what the Christian life is all about. It is more than an Old Testament Messianic prophecy. This psalm is a revelation of the essence of what life is like when lived in right relationship with Jesus Christ who said, *"I am the Good Shepherd"* (John 10:11). It is the revelation of what it's like when the Lord shepherds your life.

The chapters in this book do not put forth a scholarly exposition, but rather they are the thoughts of one pastor/under-shepherd and fellow sheep-fold dweller inspired by personal experiences that have brought fresh revelation of the reality of David's anointed song of praise which declares, *"The Lord is my Shepherd."*

May these chapters encourage every Christian to hope restored in your days of unwelcome adversity, inspire you to faith renewed in your waiting room of unanswered prayer, and empower you to exuberant praise in your moments of victory as you come to a new realization that all of your days are meant to bring to you fresh experiences which prove to you, indeed, the Lord is your Shepherd.

I pray these thoughts challenge all of us as pastors and church leaders to consider that our first, foremost and most fulfilling work and ministry is to bring to the people a revelation of the person of Jesus Christ. A revelation which flows from our own walk with the Good Shepherd and translates into the passionate purpose of all that we do in answer to the most vital of all requests ever made, *"Sir, we would see Jesus"* (John 12:21 KJV).

– Terry Kirschman

PART 1

⌒⌒⌒

BEFORE THE LORD CAN SHEPHERD YOUR LIFE

A s a prerequisite to the Lord becoming the shepherd of your life, you must have a growing relationship with Him.

A. W. Tozer said one of the tragedies of Christianity lies in the fact so many who have found Christ feel no need to further pursue Christ. The words of Jesus in Revelation have been the subject of a painted illustration that immediately comes to mind when we read this verse: *"Here I am! I stand at the door and knock! If any one hears My voice and opens the door, I will come in and eat with him and he with Me"* (Revelation 3:20).

This verse speaks of personal, intimate fellowship with Jesus. But let us not forget this invitation was first to a church; the church of Laodicea. It was a body of believers that had a name, but was spiritually dead (Revelation 3:20).

In reality, it is a picture of Jesus actually standing on the outside of His church asking to enter. And the key to the open door was the ability to hear His voice.

We experience the shepherding presence of the Lord in our lives as we make knowing Him and making Him known to others our primary, life-long pursuit. How can we make Christ known *in a living way* unless we first know Him *in a living way* and can hear His voice ourselves?

THE GIVER

America is really an oasis of God's material blessing in a world where millions search daily for just enough food to exist. I have always said that God is a blesser, not a curser. He's a giver, not a taker. And no where in the universe is this evidenced more than in America where our forefathers founded the nation and its governance upon the laws of God's Word and the Gospel of Christ.

The unbelieving third world, held in the want and despair of false religion and the oppressive rule of the "god of this world," views our prosperity with a deep envy and disdain which is fueled by more than philosophical differences. It is spiritual in nature. And yet it is precisely in the midst of God's abundant blessing where we run the greatest risk of forgetting God.

We become like eager children tearing open Christmas packages, one after the other with ravenous delight, never once thinking to give their parents a grateful glance for what it took to provide such a pile of goodies.

We must never lose sight of the Giver in the midst of all the gifts.

A WINNING LIFESTYLE

Great churches abound in America. They are great in programs, real estate holdings and gifted leaders with a motivational message which inspires an entrepreneurial spirit, bolsters self-esteem and a positive outlook on life. Thank the Lord for every denominational and independent church that is preaching the Gospel of Jesus to a lost world. And Christians, of all people, should be the example of a winning lifestyle.

The question I have is, "What is it we are really winning if not the victory over our sin nature which keeps us from being more like Jesus? For what purpose am I trying to experience the best life now and to realize my full potential if not to make Jesus known to others?" I don't accuse or criticize any. I trust this is the reason and motivation for the ministry and message of more churches than I know.

"HE GIVES YOU THE ABILITY"

Before Israel entered into the Land of Canaan, God told Moses to warn the people not to separate the material blessings He was giving to them from His presence in their midst. *"For the LORD your God is bringing you into a good land—a land with streams and pools of water, with springs flowing in the valleys and hills; a land with wheat and barley, vines and fig trees, pomegranates, olive oil and honey; a land where bread will not be scarce and you will lack nothing; a land where the rocks are iron and you can dig copper out of the hills. When you have eaten and are satisfied, praise the LORD your God for the good land He has given you. Be careful that you do not forget the LORD your God, failing to observe His commands, His laws and His decrees that I am giving you this day. Otherwise, when you eat and are satisfied, when you build fine houses and settle down, and when your herds and flocks grow large and your silver and gold increase and all you have is multiplied, then your heart will become proud and you will forget the LORD your God, who brought you out of Egypt, out of the land of slavery. He led you through the vast and dreadful desert, that thirsty and waterless land, with its venomous snakes and scorpions. He brought you water out of hard rock. He gave you manna to eat in the desert, something your fathers had never known, to humble and to test you so that in the end it might go well with you. You may say to yourself, 'My power and the strength of my hands have produced this wealth for me.' But remember the LORD your God, for it is He who gives you the ability to produce wealth, and so confirms His covenant, which He swore to your forefathers, as it is today"* (Deuteronomy 8:7-18).

In essence God was saying you can't have the blessings apart from right relationship with the "Blesser."

RAIN AFTER RAIN

When God pours out His blessings He gives us Himself. The blessings never come without His presence. Jesus spoke of this when He said, *"But seek first the kingdom of God and His righteousness, and all these things will be added unto you"* (Matthew 6:33 NKJV). The *"kingdom of God"* is simply the presence of His righteous rule.

It is a curiosity to me that in the midst of such abundance from

God, we still make prosperity, the better life and more blessings our pursuit, with ample motivation and instruction from authors and church leaders as to how to go about it.

I believe God is a *blesser* and we should *"ask the Lord for rain in the time of the latter rain"* (Zechariah 10:1 NKJV), because it is in His heart to give. And even in the hour of His blessing we should ask for more. However, God's invitation to continue to ask Him for favor when He is blessing is also that we never take for granted He is the One who shepherds our life—especially in the moments He is "raining" blessing upon us. God knows that in our fallen-ness, it is the time we are most apt to forget Him.

There is prosperity, abundance, blessing and victory promised to us through Christ in whom *"all the promises of God in Him are yes and amen"* (2 Corinthians1:20 NKJV).

LET'S GET IT RIGHT

Psalm 23 lays out an incredible description of all we are recipients of from the Lord who is our Good Shepherd. But in this first section we will look at some things I believe we must have *right* before we can experience the joy of His person and presence shepherding our life as He has promised to do.

Before the Lord can shepherd your life:
1. You must *know* the Good Shepherd *(Psalm 23:1).*
2. You must *need* the Good Shepherd (*Matthew 9:36).*
3. You must *trust* the Good Shepherd *(Psalm 23:1).*

CHAPTER ONE

⟡〜✻✻✻〜⟡

KNOWING
THE SHEPHERD

"The Lord is my Shepherd..."
—PSALM 23:1 NKJV

*Before the Lord can shepherd my life,
I must know who the Shepherd is and I must
learn to recognize His voice.*

In light of all we see happening in these exciting times of global events and world-wide church ministry, how invigorating to know there is a fresh revelation through communion with Jesus the Holy Spirit is giving to those who desire to know the Good Shepherd.

The Hebrew term "shepherd" (ra'ah) means "to tend a flock, generally to rule, to associate with as a friend." All these things the Lord does when He "shepherds" our life.

We will look at this more specifically in the next chapters. But when the term "shepherd" is applied to God it is "ro'eh" in the Hebrew and it appears 62 times in the Old Testament. The first reference was made by Jacob where he speaks of God as the *"Mighty One of Jacob...the Shepherd...the Rock of Israel..."* (Genesis 49:24).

This term "shepherd" (ro'eh) was never claimed by an Israelite king for himself. It belonged to God alone. Pagan kings would apply it to themselves in a blasphemous way and in doing so they would claim the god-like attributes which went along with the name in order to rule as a god over the people. The earthly king would claim this title that could only be a characterization of God Himself. This self-ascribed title of "shepherd" meant:

- The head of public worship
- The earthly mediator between the gods and mankind
- The center of national unity
- The supreme protector and leader of the nation
- The giver of every earthly blessing
- The dispenser of justice

King David never claimed this designation for himself, but emphatically declared, *"The Lord is my Shepherd!"* (Psalm 23:1 NKJV). Jesus, however did claim this title for Himself when He said, *"I am the Good Shepherd"* (John 10:11). He was declaring He was the fulfillment of all the description means and the Gospels give witness to the same. Jesus was saying,

- "I am the One whom Jacob spoke of in Genesis 49:24."
- "I am the 'Good' (kalos'/Greek) Shepherd; intrinsically good, goodness personified." *"God anointed Jesus of Nazareth with the Holy Spirit and power who went about doing good..."* (Acts 10:38 NKJV).
- "I am the object of worship in all the universe." *"At the name of Jesus every knee should bow, of those in heaven, and those on the earth, and those under the earth, that every tongue should confess that Jesus Christ is Lord, to the glory of God the Father"* (Philippians 2:10-11 NKJV).
- "I am the mediator between humanity and eternal God the Father." *"For there is one God and one Mediator between God and men, the man Christ Jesus..."* (1Timothy 2:5 NKJV).
- "I am the center of unity." *"That they all may be one, as You Father are in Me and I in You, that they also may be one in Us...that they may be one just as We are one"* (John 17:21-22 NKJV). *"He has become the chief cornerstone"* (1 Peter 2:7).
- "I am the supreme protector and leader of those who are my sheep." *"Now to Him who is able to keep you from stumbling, and to present you faultless before the presence*

of His glory with exceeding joy" (Jude 24 NKJV).
- "I am the giver of every blessing." *"His divine power has given us everything we need for life and godliness through our knowledge of Him who called us by His own glory and goodness"* (2 Peter 1:3-4). *"Until now you have asked nothing in My name. Ask, and you will receive that your joy may be full"* (John 16:24 NKJV).
- "I am the supreme dispenser of justice." *"For the Father judges no one but has committed all judgment to the Son"* (John 5:22). *"The Lord comes with ten thousands of His saints to execute judgment upon all..."* (Jude 14-15 NKJV).

JESUS THE FULFILLMENT OF THE PROMISE OF PSALM 23

When Jesus said "I am the Good Shepherd" He was declaring Himself to be the "star" of Psalm 23. And when David said, *"The Lord is my Shepherd"* he meant more than an allegory put to music whch compared his experience of tending sheep to how the Lord tends to us. He was saying the Lord is my "Ro'eh" in all this term signifies.

I can appreciate the artistic renderings of a kind and gentle Jesus, wind blowing His hair, staff in hand, gazing serenely down at a little wooly lamb resting securely in His arms. For that indeed does depict one aspect of the character of the Good Shepherd who communicates love, comfort and security. But such a picture can never paint the thousand words that belong to the Good Shepherd who is my "Ro'eh"!

The Holy Spirit gave David a revelation of the person of the Lord Jesus Christ and His relationship to all who would receive Him. Psalm 23 becomes then a revelation of what it is like when the Lord shepherds your life.

THE GOOD SHEPHERD IS A PERSONAL SHEPHERD

You cannot say, "The Lord is *a* shepherd," because this only puts Him on a level with Gandhi or Muhammad. Or, it is not enough to proclaim, "The Lord is *the* shepherd," for this only sets Him apart as one among others.

It is absolutely essential we are able to declare, *"The Lord is 'my' Shepherd."* Otherwise I am left with religious form but no life-changing relationship (2 Timothy 3:5). The scary thing is, I can have my religious convictions, my church membership, my denominational creed and politics, my full-time ministry, and not have the Lord (Ro'eh) as the One shepherding (ra'ah) my life!

———————

David knew that when the Lord shepherds your life it consists of a spiritual, personal and real relationship.

He followed King Saul, a very religious man who served Israel in the highest leadership role. But his failed relationship with God resulted in a failed ministry as king.

THE PROPER EMPHASIS

There is an uplifting emphasis on positive thinking, practical Christian living and books addressing keys to prosperity and success as God's people. These are wonderfully inspiring and much needed in the church today. For it is hell that deals in deficit and lack. And it is heaven which deals in prosperity and abundance. But this matter of the believer knowing the Good Shepherd and being familiar with His voice deserves more emphasis than we are giving it.

Maybe we're afraid of a "deeper life extremism," or perhaps "success and prosperity" is the itch it pays to scratch right now. Or maybe we have actually accepted the adage as truth that you can be "so heavenly minded you are no earthly good." Perhaps the real fact of the matter is that the opposite is true—until we become truly "heavenly minded" we really aren't much good for Christ's Kingdom here on earth.

STUBBLE OR SILVER?

I have asked myself this question: "While I'm busy as a pastor and under-shepherd, accomplishing the vision and mission God has given me for His church locally, am I bringing to the sheep a revelation of Jesus the *"Chief Shepherd"*? (1Peter 5:4). I believe when it's all said and done, the work of erecting church buildings, directing ministry programs and administrating church business will be either *"hay, wood and stubble"* or *"gold, sliver and precious stones"* (1 Corinthians 3:12) because we did or did not bring a revelation of Jesus to the people.

Our Lord said He would draw all manner of people to Himself if we would lift Him up (John 12:32). How important it is to know that among the many good reasons why people come to our church, the primary one is they are looking for and finding a revelation of the person of Jesus to their souls.

It is the privilege and joy of every Christian believer to be on a relational level with Jesus so as to know His voice when He speaks by His Spirit in accordance with His written Word. John said, *"As for you, the anointing you received from Him remains in you, and you do not need anyone to teach you. But as His anointing teaches you about all things and as that anointing is real, not counterfeit—just as it has taught you, remain in Him"* (1 John 2:27).

THE GOOD SHEPHERD'S VOICE CAN AND MUST BE HEARD

As a pastor, it is my conviction that part of my commitment to the pastors who serve on my staff is to value and strengthen their ministry. If I help them to succeed, I too will be successful. But this also requires a commitment on their part to cultivate a right relationship with me.

I had reached a pivotal point in one pastorate with a staff member whom I thought had breached loyalty boundaries in our relationship and I was going to approach him on the matter. I was prepared to let him go. This is never a small issue, yet I was so convinced this was the right thing to do.

I admit I hadn't spent much time in prayer concerning the matter. So before my meeting with him I figured I should cover all of my bases and I asked the Lord, "Well, what would you have me to do about this?"

Immediately the Holy Spirit spoke a Scripture passage into my mind. It was a Messianic verse which gives us a glimpse into the heart of Jesus, the Messiah: *"A bruised reed He will not break, and a smoldering wick He will not snuff out"* (Isaiah.42:3).

In that moment, when I heard the voice of the Shepherd in His Word speak to my heart, I not only received a revelation of how Jesus would respond, I had a glimpse of the real issues in this staff member's life. At that point in time, he was a bruised reed emotionally and a smoldering wick so far as his ministry confidence was concerned.

My wrong response is all it would take to break his spirit and quench his desire to follow the Lord's call in ministry. The wrong response would be to fire him. Eventually he resigned and moved on, but to this day he and his lovely wife are our friends and they are one of the most dedicated and talented couples in full-time ministry with whom we still maintain contact.

DO YOU KNOW HIS VOICE?

For the sake of people's lives, including their emotional, relational and spiritual well being, the Good Shepherd's voice can and must be heard. I believe Jesus understood the danger of His children not getting this right when He emphasized the importance of knowing Him and hearing His voice. *"All whoever came before Me were thieves and robbers, but the sheep did not listen to them...I am the Good Shepherd; I know my sheep and my sheep know me...I have other sheep that are not of this sheep pen. I must bring them also, They too will listen to My voice and there shall be one flock and one shepherd...My sheep listen to My voice; I know them and they follow Me"* (John 10:8,14,16,27).

Jesus also warned there would be other voices which would come and that we would need discernment through familiarity with Him to distinguish His voice from theirs. *"For false christs and false prophets will appear and perform great signs and miracles to deceive even the elect if that were possible"* (Matthew 24:24).

The word "christ" (christos/Greek) means "anointed." Jesus didn't say that in the last days there would be those coming claiming to be Him personally. He said they would come claiming to be an "anointed" one. But this anointing would be false.

Whether it was an anointing which comes from a demonic spirit attacking the church from without, or just a persuasive charismatic human spirit "ministering" and seducing the church from within, the point is it would be a false anointing because it wasn't the Holy Spirit's anointing. The glory of Jesus would not be central and a revelation of Jesus would not be prevalent. Knowing the Shepherd is the only way to discern the difference.

Before the Lord can shepherd my life I have to know who He is. I have to know Him personally. I have to be in right relationship with Him. I have to have a capacity to hear His voice in His Word by His Spirit.

I must be willing to go where He is taking me. Jesus made this very clear when He said, *"I am the Good Shepherd; I know My sheep and they know Me...My sheep listen to my voice; I know them and they follow Me"* (John 10:14,27).

This almost sounds so elementary that it doesn't need to be stated. However, how many people attending churches across America really don't have a vital relationship with the Lord, their Good Shepherd? And the direction of their lives is proof of this. I have encountered such people in the churches I have pastored. They are fine individuals who attend church regularly and give money and time to be involved in the ministry program of the church. Yet, they are making decisions and demonstrating attitudes and character in stark contrast to the person of Jesus as revealed in the Gospels. They display a noticeable "lack of likeness" to The Shepherd and seem to "go places" where He would never lead them.

CHRIST'S SHEPHERDING INFLUENCE IS SEEN IN OUR LIVES

In a church where I pastored for several years, I encountered something which caught me completely by surprise. Having been raised in a Pentecostal minister's home and in church all of my life, I thought I had seen just about everything. I felt I was rather well prepared to fulfill the Lord's pastoral leadership call upon my life. However, one Sunday I was preaching on the Spirit of God as the *"breath"* of God which is the word given in both the Greek and

17

Hebrew. I made a statement about man being created a living soul by the breath of God (Genesis 2:7).

I went on to state that's what distinguishes us from every other living creature God has made. The Creator has not only given mankind physical life ("bios"/Greek), but He has also given him an eternal spirit with the capacity to know God and live in His presence forever. This is what comes to life at new birth. It is what happened to the disciples after Jesus' resurrection appearance *to* them when He breathed *on* them and said, *"Receive the Holy Spirit"* (John 20:22).

Then on the heels of this I said, off-the-cuff and in a light humorous manner, "I'm sorry if your pet puppy has died, but chances are you'll not see little 'FiFi' in heaven."

That week our hospital visitation chaplain came to me and said, "Pastor I don't know what to do about all the phone calls I'm receiving in protest to what you said about pets not going to heaven!"

He even forwarded an email sent to him which referred to a website sponsored by a mainline denomination listing several scriptures as "proof texts" indicating pets go to heaven. I took a few hours that week and in defense of my off-the-cuff remark, I wrote a brief commentary on the texts from that website and made copies available at the church visitor's desk. They were all gone before church was over the following Sunday.

I was startled at how concerned some were at the thought their pets weren't going to heaven, and yet I wondered who they had invited to church lately or at least demonstrated the love of Christ to someone who didn't know the Savior. I wondered upon what basis they thought their pets were getting into heaven.

Somehow I just couldn't bring myself to accept that the Lord's shepherding influence in my life would incite me to insist my dog or cat go to heaven while my neighbor went to hell—not knowing the Savior for lack of a loving witness from me. This concern includes pastors and church leaders.

SPIRITUAL CONVICTIONS?

In another church I pastored, one man who was a former minister was elected to the deacon board. No longer in pastoral ministry, he now had the wonderful privilege of standing in support of pastoral leadership and in agreement with others to see God's destiny for the church accomplished. Instead, his biggest struggle was the fact that when communion was served it was white grape juice and not red.

When He was told that white grape juice was used so as to not leave spill stains on clothing or church furnishings, he would not be dissuaded from his opinion. He was willing to serve communion to others, he said, but refused to partake himself because it was the wrong color.

Somehow I just couldn't bring myself to accept that the Lord's shepherding influence in my life would inspire me to rally the cause of correctly-colored grape juice, or rally the cause of categorizing the musical styles God "loves" and the ones He "hates, or discriminating between social classes or ethnic groups we will include or exclude from our church's ministry outreach program. And the list of "spiritual convictions" goes on.

What I am talking about is that before the Lord can shepherd our lives, you and I must be committed to knowing Him and listening to His voice and following Him even to places and people beyond our proverbial "comfort zones." If this is happening then there will be evidence of such in my values, attitudes, decisions, and the general direction my life is going.

I am not speaking of moral or sinless perfection, rather I am referring to a general direction of maturity and Christ-likeness my life is taking which comes from the living Lord shepherding my daily walk.

A "TRIUMPHAL PROCESSION"

The issue is not that we have problems. The question is, do we have the same problems we had last year? Paul says the impact of the Good Shepherd's leading us is always to triumph and the result is that a knowledge of Him is manifested to others through us. *"But thanks be to God who always leads us in triumphal procession in Christ and through us spreads everywhere the fragrance of the knowledge of Him"* (2 Corinthians 2:14).

If I know Him, then through my life the knowledge of Him will be manifested to others. Before the Lord can shepherd my life, I have to know the Shepherd who is Lord.

CHAPTER TWO

NEEDING THE GOOD SHEPHERD

*"But when He saw the multitudes He was moved
with compassion for them, because they were weary and
scattered, like sheep having no shepherd..."*
– MATTHEW 9:36 NKJV

*I contend before the Lord can shepherd our lives,
we all must come to the realization that on our best day, and at
our strongest point, in the midst of our greatest blessings and
successes, we are still no more than vulnerable sheep needing to
know, hear and follow the Good Shepherd.*

No matter where you live in the world, people look to be led and cared for. Even in America with the emphasis upon rugged individualism governed by a democracy "of the people, by the people and for the people," we still look more and more to our leaders for direction and provision. It is human nature and also a spiritual need in the church.

THE MISPLACED SENSE OF NEED

Is my desire for the Lord's shepherding presence a daily "felt need"?

My greatest influence as a pastor is not through any talents and gifts I may possess—as important assets as they are to effective leadership. It is by my personal need for Christ's shepherding presence that I am willing to openly role model.

As gifted and powerfully anointed leader as the apostle Paul was, I believe this is part of what he meant when he said, *"Imitate me, just as I also imitate Christ"* (1Corinthians 11:1 NKJV). In this way I am constantly leading souls to Jesus and together we are *"the people of His pasture, the sheep of His hand"* (Psalm 95:7 NKJV) and our *"expectation is from Him"* (Psalm 62:5 NKJV).

What is really needed is a healthy understanding of the ministry of the Good Shepherd to pastor His church, one sheep at a time. I can be in the church and not *"in Christ"* (1 Corinthians 1:30; Acts 17:28; Romans 8:9). I can be in Christ and not be familiar with the voice of the Good Shepherd.

The less I personally look to Jesus, the more I will look to church leadership or church programming for the provision of nurture and care for my soul in ways that really is the ministry of Jesus my Good Shepherd. This is what I call a sense of need "misplaced."

I had the chance during a brief sabbatical from the senior pastorate to attend a number of great interdenominational churches in California. They are some of the most successful in attendance, programming, staffing, facilities, contemporary musical worship, outreach and church planting in America. The many thousands who attend these truly outstanding churches are on the receiving end of sound Biblical teaching utilizing the multi-media technology our culture expects. In fact, today when deciding on a home church there are many who will not attend if the facility does not have a website. To them it is an indication the church does not communicate on their level.

All we can do to be culturally relevant in communicating the Gospel is obligatory. The message is always sacred, but the methods never are. However the methodology, programming and ministry philosophy to attract people to the church and even embrace them into membership are not enough unless church members and attendees are learning to know the Good Shepherd's voice and their desire for Him is a felt need every day. *"The LORD is near to all who call on Him, to all who call on Him in truth"* (Psalm 145:18 NKJV). *"Come near to God and He will come near to you..."* (James 4:8).

DIFFERENT NEEDS

On his telecast, "The Potter's House," I heard Bishop T. D. Jakes preach a sermon entitled, "The Spell Breaker." He shed light on this issue when he addressed the fact that some go to church to be entertained and others to be delivered. Some attend the house of God to get excited and others to be edified. Still others go to church just to be "numbed" into forgetting their problems for a short while.

It is true people do have different needs. Affluent communities don't usually need a church with a drug rehabilitation program. They need a support group providing some free time and social outlet for new moms, or Bible studies for young professionals. There are differences in "seekers," but it's not just between personal taste in the way people like to have church. It also has to do with whether or not we are cultivating a desire to know the Lord through a vital walk in the Spirit whom Jesus said would *"testify of Me"* (John 15:26).

When you are not familiar with the voice of the Good Shepherd, it is only natural to seek to find all you need in a sermon, a teaching, a church program or at least the healthier social environment a church can offer. In this case we have misplaced our vital sense of need upon the church and it's leadership more than the Shepherd of our life.

I suggest that in the wonderful return to church by "seekers" at every level of society, we need to discover the Holy Spirit in His fullness is "seeker friendly" too. Without a doubt one cannot serve Christ without helping people. Jesus said that the visible essence of Christian living is demonstrated in responding to human need. *"For*

I was hungry and you gave Me something to eat, I was thirsty and you gave Me something to drink, I was a stranger and you invited Me in, I needed clothes and you clothed Me, I was sick and you looked after Me, I was in prison and you came to visit Me. Then the righteous will answer Him, 'Lord, when did we see You hungry and feed You, or thirsty and give You something to drink? When did we see You a stranger and invite You in, or needing clothes and clothe You? When did we see You sick or in prison and go to visit You?' The King will reply, 'I tell you the truth, whatever you did for one of the least of these brothers of Mine, you did for Me'" (Matthew 25:35-40).

WHO IS YOUR SOURCE?

One of the greatest goals of every church is to identify the needs of the community it is located in and then develop practical ministry programming to meet those needs, demonstrating the love of Christ so we can earn the right in their minds to speak to them of *"the love of Christ that constrains us"* (2 Corinthians.5:14 KJV).

In my opinion, the greatest churches in America are those such as "The Church Without Walls" in Tampa, Florida, "First Assembly of God" in Phoenix, Arizona, "Trinity Church" and "Peacemakers Ministries" of Miami, Florida and "Times Square Church" of New York City, that are effectively meeting practical human need through creative ministry approaches in order to gain an opportunity to communicate the Gospel of Christ. But what I am speaking about is the issue of parishioners looking to church leadership for what they can only find in their relationship with the Lord Jesus.

――――――――――

As people come to Christ and learn to hear His voice, their felt need for the Lord will deepen. As they turn to Him daily, the Good Shepherd will lead them into "green pastures" of His blessing and provision as they do His will.

I would suggest that in some ways the politics of how we go about doing "church business" contributes to the problem of "misplaced need" and expectations which are fostered in the minds of church members.

"GOD'S MAN"

The following scenario is certainly not the status quo in the majority of denominational churches. But at the same time it is not at all uncommon. For instance when searching for a place of ministry to serve as the Lord's under-shepherds, pastoral candidates' resumés clearly spell out their leadership success stories, highlighting the valued qualities for effective leadership that they possess, presenting themselves as potentially "God's man for the job."

Case in point: A pastor friend of mine who was unhappy with his place in ministry at the time, once insinuated to me I must have embellished my resumé so as to obtain an invitation to pastor the church where I currently was serving. He had apparently obtained a copy of my resumé from somewhere and I guess he didn't think it was representative of the Terry Kirschman he thought he knew. Or at least in his estimate I certainly didn't deserve to be in the position I was in.

When he eventually received a call from a church, he complimented me as having given him the idea of including "a philosophy of ministry" section in his resumé, which he said was "just the thing" which attracted the pulpit committee's attention.

POLITICAL MANEUVERINGS

Pastors are hired by church boards and ratified by a vote of the majority of the membership. It is done this way in some denominations because it can work if there is a praying congregation involved—and, it does seem the way to go about "church business" in a democratic society. However, based upon the job history and ministry record that has been established and promoted to the members on behalf of the pastoral candidate, certain expectations of what should now happen in the church because of the new pastor are formed in the minds of congregations.

Once a pastor has been "hired," church members will often still vote their approval or disapproval of his job performance again a year or two down the road, after they've had a little time to see their shepherd "in action."

They do this in what is called a confirmation vote by the corporate members. By then, if there are still those who stand in opposition of the new pastor the first power struggles begin to surface. In reality, what is at work in the church is a "democratic/religious/corporate" organizational hybrid, complete with political maneuverings, campaigning, church foyer and parking lot lobbyists, and of course prayer "caucus" meetings asking for the Lord's "blessing" or "divine intervention," depending of course which side of the issues you are on.

WHO BUILDS THE CHURCH?

Speaking of prayer "caucus" meetings, my wife received a phone call from a dear church member one day. This friend was very upset because she had just received a phone call from the wife of the senior pastor whom I had followed. This pastor's wife had related to her that some people were not happy with the new pastor's ministry and she and her husband had been agreeing with the discontents, and together they were "praying" us out of the church.

The senior pastor is called upon to wear many hats including; teacher, fundraiser, vision-caster, counselor, preacher, CEO, staff enabler, personal friend, and more. And in some ways the congregation votes indirectly with respect to the pastor's approval rating every time the offering plate goes by. So the temptation a pastor may face is for the "ministry to follow the money" so to speak.

When this happens we have forgotten who it is that really pays the bills after all. It is Jesus, the Good Shepherd who said He would build His church and the gates of hell would not prevail against it (Matthew16:18). The program of "building" includes every aspect.

The church is more than a corporate body, it is *His* body (Ephesians 5:30). His blessing, not our work is what truly makes ministry a success.

In situations like these we may offer many wonderful people-helping ministry programs—which is every local church's responsibility and opportunity to have effective ministry. But what we have constructed are churches whose most urgent requirements, if they are going to stay in operation, always seem to be more money and a charismatic or popular leader who can effectively appease and balance the influence of the "power brokers" in the church. Why should this be if the Good Shepherd's voice is being heard in His church?

THE INDISPENSABLE REVELATION OF CHRIST THE GOOD SHEPHERD

One of the issues which arose in the early church had the potential of disrupting its mission and splintering its fellowship into warring factions. Certainly the voice of the Good Shepherd needed to be heard. When addressing defining doctrinal statements with regards to the Gentile believers who were coming into the nearly all-Jewish church, the voice of the Spirit and the mind of Christ were sought in prayer.

History bears out how the right choice was made and the statement of what the basis for the final decision was is recorded in Acts 15:28 NKJV: *"For it seemed good to the Holy Spirit and to us."*

The voice of the Spirit had been heard and the testimony of Jesus to His church had been heeded. Even though pastors presenting their credentials and record of qualifying experience for congregational review is a legitimate part of the leadership decision-making process, the real challenge is to live up to it in a way which doesn't distract people from looking unto Jesus, their Good Shepherd, Author and Perfecter, Leader and Instructor of their faith (Hebrews 12:2).

I see the ministry of leadership being to lead God's people to look together to Jesus, the Chief Shepherd of the flock, for the answers in individual lives and the corporate life of the church.

The revelation of Christ the Good Shepherd is indispensable.

HEARING THE VOICE BEHIND THE VOICE

In the likeness of Jesus the Good Shepherd who is also "Prophet, Priest and King," under-shepherd's are called to function in both priestly and prophetic ministry.

Most every church attendee wants a "priest"—one who stands before God petitioning in behalf of the needs of the people. But it is by far the minority that gets jazzed about a "prophet"—one who stands before the people in behalf of God, speaking the heart and mind of Christ to His church.

But unless the prophetic functions through church leadership and people are taught that they can hear the voice of the Savior, where is the testimony of Jesus? For *"the testimony of Jesus is the spirit of prophecy"* (Revelation 19:10 NKJV).

Prophetic ministry flows from our own walk with Jesus. It doesn't come from any other source.

It is a vital part of the prophetic in pastoral ministry that when from our relationship with the Good Shepherd we hear His voice speak to us a word for those to whom we are called to minister. It is imperative we are willing to teach, preach, and speak it so people's hearts will burn with the revelation to their souls the Holy Spirit will bring. The result will be they are inspired to know more of His speaking voice in their continual walk with Him.

THE PLACE OF THE PROPHETIC

Rev. Yonggi Cho, of Seoul, Korea, pastor of one of the world's largest congregations, stated, "churches are built more so by prophecy than by program." I interpret this as being a vision birthed in the heart of a pastor by the Holy Spirit as God's mission and destiny for that church—and the vision is sustained by the prophetic through his life and ministry.

The prophetic must function in a leader's life if the church is going to hear the voice of the Good Shepherd. It can be quenched by church "politics," which I would define as doing God's work man's way by putting a spiritual mask on our own personal agenda.

I believe this is one of the truths revealed in the account of Ananias and Sapphira in Acts 5. When this happens, we settle for church "busy work." But a spiritual void is the result and supernatural results in people's lives are few and far between.

In such cases, believers are not inspired to hear the Good Shepherd's voice on a daily basis, but rather look forward to the next sermon the pastor will deliver. The prophetic in our preaching and teaching on Sunday is to inspire desire in the hearts of people to hear the voice of the Good Shepherd on a personal level on Monday, Tuesday and throughout the week.

This becomes a challenge because "control freaks" in the church get quite nervous with leadership in the pulpit who is not only serving as priest but also willing to minister as prophet in this way.

Before the Lord can shepherd our lives, God's people need to look to Him first and foremost in every situation for His shepherding influence.

A pastor can do many things, but he can never be the substitute for the Lord's guidance. James says we can grieve the Holy Spirit's work in our life when our outlook cultivates a response based upon a carnal value system. James calls it friendship with the world. *"Anyone who chooses to be a friend of the world becomes an enemy of God. Or do you think that Scripture says without reason that the Spirit He caused to live in us envies intensely?"* (James 4:4-5).

The Holy Spirit is envious of everything we look to *first*, at the expense of trusting His work and ministry in us and on our behalf. This can include unrealistic expectations of church leadership and one another.

DON'T SELL YOURSELF SHORT

The following example illustrates how easy it is for us to look to the world's solution for our challenges in life before we do the Holy Spirit of God who dwells within us.

A dear woman in a church where I was a staff member came to my office one day asking about the possibility of using hypnosis to help her lose some weight. I tried to remind her that one of the aspects of the Holy Spirit's fruit in her life was self-control.

I encouraged her to trust the Lord in prayer to give her the discipline and grace to pursue a healthy diet and exercise program under a doctor's care for the best results. In the process, time spent in prayer and the Word could give the Holy Spirit opportunity to speak personal promise into her life.

29

How often God's people sell themselves short and cut themselves off from the Spirit's ministry not realizing this is part of the Lord's shepherding influence in their lives.

WEARY AND SCATTERED FOR LACK OF THE GOOD SHEPHERD

Matthew records that when Jesus looked upon the crowd following Him, what He saw were people whose condition could only be met by His personal ministry to them as the Good Shepherd. His description of their condition was far more than any one disciple, apostle or ministry program the church could create to deal with effectively.

This description includes more than just the crowd on that particular day. It is the revelation of *any* life lived without the experience of His personal shepherding presence.

Jesus saw them as *"weary"* (eskulmenoi/Greek) meaning; "faint, on the verge of collapse, harassed."

When a person faints they even stop breathing for a few seconds. It is the picture of life lived without moral and spiritual strength, on the verge of physical and emotional collapse.

FULFILLMENT AND PURPOSE

There is no real spiritual, moral or emotional strength enough to endure the harassment of spiritual forces and adverse circumstances we will encounter in this world apart from Christ's shepherding influence. It will be increasingly so as we approach the culmination of human history and the return of the Lord according to Bible prophecy (Revelation.12:12).

One hundred years ago a heart attack was a rare occurrence. Today it is the number one killer. The leading prescribed medications by doctors relate to depression, anxiety or address an inability to cope in some way. Jesus saw them *"scattered"* (rhip'to/Greek). It means "a thoughtless dispersion; a pointless, helter-skelter, indiscriminate directionless movement." It is the picture of life lived without the fulfillment and purpose only a living relationship with Jesus can bring.

For us to know such fulfillment and purpose we must *know* and

30

fulfill the *purposes* Jesus has spoken to us about. And although being in fellowship and in right relationship with others in a local church is the best place for this to happen, no pastor or church program can be the source for the vision and mission for your life. This only comes from a personal relationship with Jesus—when you have learned to hear and to know His voice.

A LIFE-LONG COMMUNION

"Scattered" is also the picture of life being influenced from external influences like startled sheep who run with the flock in fear of a noise, or are just being swayed to graze in the direction the wind might be blowing. Paul said the role of the leadership gifts Jesus has imparted to His church are for the *"...equipping of the saints for the work of the ministry, for the edifying of the body of Christ, till we all come to the unity of the faith and of the knowledge of the Son of God, to a perfect man, to the measure of the stature of the fullness of Christ, that we should no longer be children, tossed to and fro and carried about with every wind of doctrine, by the trickery of men, in the cunning craftiness of deceitful plotting..."* (Ephesians 4:11-14 NKJV).

I believe Paul is saying that if sheep are going to cease from being scattered, leadership must direct them to *"the knowledge of the Son of God,"* a personal encounter and life-long communion with the Good Shepherd—a felt need every day of their lives. Paul says, *"For when I am weak, then I am strong"* (2 Corinthians 12:10 NKJV).

Before the Lord can shepherd my life I must be willing to admit that *"scattered"* and *"weary"* is a good description without His shepherding influence, no matter how wonderful the church is I attend.

I must be willing to live joyously and powerfully in the freedom of need; needing the Lord's shepherding presence, admitting that a day without communion with Him is an assertion of my prideful independence and a boast against Him.

CHAPTER THREE

⌘~⦚⦚⦚⦚~⦚

TRUSTING THE
GOOD SHEPHERD

"The Lord is my shepherd, I shall not be in want."
– PSALM 23:1

Before the Lord can shepherd my life,
I must be ready to accept His provision and
be willing to submit to His leading.

T he Lord is always—and in every way—completely trustworthy. As we have mentioned, the Shepherd by definition of the Hebrew term "ro'eh" is, the protector and leader of all who are His. He is the giver of every good blessing. Being the Good (kalos/Greek) Shepherd, He is intrinsically good. Meaning He is the embodiment of all that is beneficial, valuable and morally praiseworthy. He is excellent in nature and His character is one of purity of heart and life.

THE CROSS: PROOF OF
CHRIST'S TRUSTWORTHINESS AND
RIGHTS TO OWNERSHIP

But more than this, Jesus said, *"I am the Good Shepherd. The Good Shepherd lays down His life for the sheep"* (John 10:11). This supreme act is what makes Jesus supremely worthy of our trust. And the Holy Spirit further records this also is His claim to ownership upon our lives. Paul says, *"...you are not your own; you were bought at a price"* (1Corinthians.6:19-20).

Trust says if He is intrinsically good, supremely trustworthy and has claimed ownership of my life at the price of His own blood, having bought back my life from the slave market of sin after I had sold it so cheaply, and if I belong to Him on those terms, then I can trust Him to take care of what belongs to Him.

Trust settles the issue of ownership and then lives, thinks and acts accordingly.

The Good Shepherd can, by rights of ownership, do with His sheep as He pleases. Trust understands that whether it is what I would choose or not, whatever He does with me will result for good because He cannot do otherwise.

GRACE: THE FOUNDATION OF TRUST

The foundation of trust in Christ is His sacrifice at the cross which is the display of His gift of grace.

Everything about my life has to do with His grace. The enemy of trust and the despiser of grace is self and pride. Even the refusal to accept by faith the grace of God in Christ because it is just too incomprehensible is pride—because I am proud of my ability to comprehend it before I will accept.

The foundation of faith is grace. *"For it is by grace you have been saved, through Faith"* (Ephesians 2:8). My faith to petition God in accordance with the promises of His Word has to do with grace because I don't deserve the least of His favors. But my asking has nothing to do with what I deserve, rather it has to do with His grace and what He has determined to give and to do in my behalf. And it is because of His grace that He invites us to: *"open your mouth wide and I will fill it"* (Psalm.81:10 NKJV).

The God of grace and power is never honored by the smallness of our requests. Those who live in His grace enjoy the freedom to ask largely of the Lord because His grace is the foundation of their confident trust. The thing which destroys trust and erodes faith is self and pride and the resulting sinful responses which break our fellowship with the *"God of all grace"* (1 Peter 5:10).

David said that when the Lord shepherds my life *"I shall not be in want."* *"Want"* (chacer/Hebrew) means; "to lack, to be abated, cut back or decreased, to cause to fail, to be made lower."

When the Lord is my Shepherd, life's meaning, significance and purpose will not be abated, cut back, decreased or made less.

It is more than just *not* lacking temporal needs. It has to do with life lived in the fulfillment of my eternal destiny and the contentment which comes from knowing that when He shepherds me I will not fail.

"I WILL NOT WANT"

Let me illustrate. When I speak of walking in the grace of Christ's shepherding influence we receive when we trust the Good Shepherd completely, I'm talking about Reneé, a brilliant and beautiful woman with a promising career. She was a young wife and mother of two who was in the hospital recovering from major cancer surgery when my wife and I visited her.

The surgical procedure included a double mastectomy and a complete hysterectomy. We went there to encourage Reneé and her mother Yvonne, who herself had already gone through several major cancer surgeries. And in the last year she had recovered from a near death encounter with a rare blood disease that required the application of experimental medications as a final resort to spare her life.

Reneé was not just recovering from surgery, she was also waiting for her biopsy report. Then she would know what the days ahead would look like for her from a medical point of view. As we conversed with these two dear friends, it became evident that even in Reneé's weakened physical condition and on a morphine drip, her trust in the Lord was anything but faint.

Her response to our heart-felt expressions of concern was simply as follows. "Unbelievers would ask how can God allow something like this to occur. Some Christians would wonder why is this happening to me and not to someone else whose lifestyle would bring more susceptibility to this kind of thing. But I'm looking forward to seeing all the good the Lord is going to bring out of this in my life and in the lives of others who I care about and who know me."

Yvonne said, "It's amazing to see how the Lord shepherds your life every day and the detailed events He orchestrates to bring the right doctors and nurses into our life at the right time, even to the point of getting us this perfect room right across from the nurse's station. It even has a sleeper sofa that allows me to spend the nights here with Reneé. The room is also the first one off of the elevators so Reneé's son, Jordon, doesn't have to walk too far to see his mom."

Jordon just so happened to be Reneé's handsome, thirteen year old son who was diagnosed with a radical cancerous tumor on his spine. His recent surgery had left him paralyzed on one side and so walking was difficult. Not to mention the chemotherapy which had taken all of his beautiful black hair, left him with dark shadows around his eyes and sapped him of his youthful energy.

Reneé observed, "We think the Shriners hospital will take Jordon for rehabilitation. And since we were wondering how much time Jordon may have left, the good news is that they wouldn't consider taking any young person if they hadn't been given at least a year to live."

Incidentally, Reneé was also in the middle of a very difficult divorce!

"The Lord is my shepherd, I shall not be in want." The Reneés and the Yvonnes in our world are some of life's best illustrations of the meaning of this verse. In other words, in the midst of the worst events this life and hell itself can seemingly throw at me, I will not lack what I am in need of, and neither will my destiny, fulfillment and purpose for the glory of God be abated, cut back or decreased.

In this I will not fail because the "Ro'eh" who is "the embodiment of all that is beneficial, excellent in nature, pure in heart, protector, leader, giver of every good blessing," is shepherding my life.

RIGHT RELATIONSHIPS: THE ENVIRONMENT FOR A GROWING TRUST IN GOD

God's Word is the promise and the proving of our trusting relationship with Him. Jesus said, *"If you love Me you will obey what I command"* (John 14:15).

When we obey His Word, the Lord makes good on His promises. I have thought about this command to obedience and how it relates to

36

loving Christ in this way. When I want to express my love to my spouse or my friends, there are many ways I can communicate my feelings: gifts, thoughtful actions, kind words, forgiveness, an embrace, a kiss, etc. Some day in a glorified body I will stand in the Lord's presence and I anticipate not only bowing down before Him, but also embracing Him. But right now in this world, the one and only way I can express my love to the Lord who is present only by His Spirit, is through trust which obeys.

When David says, *"...we are the people of His pasture and the sheep of His hand"* (Psalm.95:7), he is speaking of trust in the context of our interpersonal relationships as well. David says *"we"* ('anachnuw/Hebrew) together are the people of His *"pasture"* (mir'yth/Hebrew).

It is the picture of a flock feeding together in a pasture, *"People"* ('am/Hebrew) signifies more than just a religious gathering. It stands for "persons who are countrymen; those who are kindred." We belong to Him and also to one another.

―――――――○※∰※○―――――――

When God desires to bless you He always sends a person into your life. It is in the context of our right relationships with one another that we are encouraged to trust the Lord.

What God has done for you He can do for me because together we are His people. If you are in right relationship with others, testimonies of God's blessing and provision won't discourage you when *your* blessing has not yet arrived. It will encourage you to trust.

RIGHT RELATIONSHIPS

How many times has the testimony of God's love, and faithfulness from others, been what has encouraged your trust in the Lord?

Right relationships with one another in the body of Christ is a good indication we are in right relationship with the Lord. The opposite is also true. We have a tendency to treat others the way we are treating the Lord, or perceive Him to be treating us.

When relationships are not right at home or in the church it is anything but trust in God which is fostered. James says, *"For where envy and self-seeking (strife) exist, confusion and every evil thing (work) are there"* (James 3:16 NKJV).

In such an environment of distrust of one another, confusion concerning the ways of God is certainly generated. There is no telling what may be manifested as part of the *"every evil work"* James says is also present. For example, how many people have fallen away from the Lord and left the church because deep disappointment and discouragement in broken relationships resulted in hurt and distrust which cast a cloud of confusion and doubt in their life? And it was enough for them to break fellowship with the church and with the Lord.

In an atmosphere where trust was broken between members of Christ's church, they became confused about trust in God. In those times the tactic of the enemy is always to impugn the character of God to the hurting and discouraged in order to set in motion "every evil work."

"STRENGTH AND POWER"

When David says we are the "sheep of His hand," he is speaking of more than a friendly, good-hearted shepherd handing out a nourishing snack like one would give treats to their pet. *"Hand"* (yad/Hebrew) also signifies "strength and power."

This is the same word used when God moved upon Egypt's livestock in the fifth plague. *"...behold the hand of the Lord will be upon your cattle in the field, on the horses, on the oxen, and on the camels, and on the donkeys and on the sheep...* (Exodus.9:3 NKJV).

It is the same word used when Joshua led Israel into Canaan, miraculously crossing the Jordon River where memorial stones were set up to remember the event. Joshua said, *"That all of the peoples of the earth may know the hand of the Lord, that it is mighty, that you may fear the Lord your God forever"* (Joshua. 4:24 NKJV).

It is also the same term used when David decided to trust God's discipline in his life rather than the justice of man. *"And David said to God, 'I am in great distress. Please let us fall into the hand of the Lord, for His mercies are great; but do not let me fall into the hand of*

38

man'" (2 Samuel 24:14 NKJV).

Ezekiel describes the leading of the Lord, the revelations and visions he received and the prophetic words he spoke as being the result of the *"hand of the Lord"* upon him (Ezekiel 1:3; 3:14,22; 33:22; 37:1).

Jesus said the power of God revealed in answered prayer and His presence manifested is especially available to those who come together in agreement. *"Again, I tell you that if two of you on earth agree about anything you ask for, it will be done for you by My Father in heaven. For where two or three come together in My name, there am I with them"* (Matthew 18:19-20).

"Agree" (sumphoneo) in the Greek sounds a lot like our word symphony and that's precisely what it means: "to be suitable, harmonious, in accord, to make a pact."

This promise of answered prayer and the manifest presence of the Lord is not given just to those who want the same thing from the Almighty no matter how loud they shout or intensely they ask. We can desire the same things from God in a worship service or prayer meeting but still not talk to each other when the meeting is over!

―――――――――― ⌁⌁⌁ ――――――――――

This means not only to be in agreement with what we are asking for from the Lord, but that we are also committed to a suitable, harmonious relationship in the Lord.

We can deceive many people because man looks on the outward appearance. But we can never fool the One who answers prayer, because He looks upon the heart. As the *"sheep of His hand,"* the power and strength of the Good Shepherd is made available to us in defense against our enemies, and proactively to accomplish great things in our life.

Trusting the Lord for what He has promised is nurtured and encouraged in an environment of right relationships together as "the people of His pasture."

PART II

WHEN THE LORD SHEPHERDS YOUR LIFE

I n Psalm 23, the Holy Spirit gives us a picture of the incarnation. By the Hebrew definitions of the term *"shepherd"* (ro'eh/ra'ah), it is a picture of divinity condescending to humanity in love, friendship and authority.

The *"Shepherd"* (ro'eh) who is the head of public worship, the earthly mediator between God and man, the center of unity, the supreme protector and leader of His people, the giver of every earthly blessing and the dispenser of justice, condescends to *"shepherd"* (ra'ah) my life by tending to, ruling and associating with me as a friend.

1. He tends to the needs and wants of my life.
"So do not worry, saying, 'What shall we eat?' or 'What shall we drink?' or 'What shall we wear?' For the pagans run after all these things, and your heavenly Father knows that you need them" (Matthew 6:31-32).
"Who satisfies your desires with good things..." (Psalm 103:5).
"He fulfills the desires of those who fear Him; He hears their cry and saves them" (Psalm 145:19).

41

2. He rules in my life and over the events of my life in love and righteousness.

"But God demonstrates His own love for us in this: While we were still sinners, Christ died for us" (Romans 5:8).

"I will betroth you to Me forever; I will betroth you in righteousness and justice, in love and compassion. I will betroth you in faithfulness, and you will acknowledge the LORD" (Hosea 2:19-20).

"And we know that in all things God works for the good of those who love Him, who have been called according to His purpose" (Romans 8:28).

"For Christ's love compels us, because we are convinced that One died for all, and therefore all died. And He died for all, that those who live should no longer live for themselves but for Him who died for them and was raised again" (2 Corinthians 5:14-15).

"You answer us with awesome deeds of righteousness..." (Psalm 65:5).

3. He associates with me as a friend and brother.

"...There is a friend who sticks closer than a brother" (Proverbs 18:24).

"I no longer call you servants, because a servant does not know his master's business. Instead, I have called you friends, for everything that I learned from My Father. I have made known to you" (John 15:15).

Both the One who makes men holy and those who are made holy are of the same family. So Jesus is not ashamed to call them brothers" (Hebrews 2:11).

DIVINELY INSPIRED

Indeed, Psalm 23 is much more than a poetic, musical allegory. David was writing revelation which came to Him from the Holy Spirit. It is a divinely inspired unveiling of the wonders of the incarnation as being more than just providing legal payment for the sins of humanity. It is the wonder of God entering into our world to shepherd our lives in order that He might bring *"many sons to glory"* (Hebrews 2:10).

In the following chapters we will consider the promises God gives to us when we make knowing, needing and trusting the Good Shepherd the pursuit of our lives. We will discover it is His shepherding presence that makes human life more than biological existence. It is what gives life the present significance God created it to have. And it is life in preparation for an eternity with God which the human mind is incapable of comprehending.

CHAPTER FOUR

‿‿‿✦✦✦✦‿‿

FINDING PEACE
AND REST

"He makes me lie down in green pastures"
– PSALM 23:2

W hen was the last time you spent a "care free" day?

Just the sheer demands everyday responsibilities press upon most of us virtually makes it a human impossibility. Not to mention the social pathologies of our time that prey upon our thoughts and emotions—if not our very lives.

Natural disasters including the earthquake and tsunami which claimed over 200,000 lives in Indonesia, India and the surrounding region defy our comprehension. And who would have imagined the need for law enforcement to enact a new nationwide warning system known as the "Amber Alert" to solicit the public's assistance in rescuing children from the clutches of predators on a regular basis.

We live our daily lives against the backdrop of a terrorist threat from radical Muslims and other enemies of western civilization of unimaginable consequence. Economic uncertainty caused by ties to the ever changing climate of international business and trade, the shifting of focus and interest in the business and labor field influenced by technological advances, along with the ever increasing cost of living is an environment which can leave our minds and hearts wrung out.

Drug addiction and alcoholism become the conditions for millions who choose to chemically numb their anxiety and medicate their pain.

ENEMIES OF OUR WELL-BEING

Stress has become big business for the pharmaceutical industry. Some estimates state that 80% of all patients in the hospital are there because of psychosomatic related illness. This means the body begins to break down under mental and emotional strain and physical illness results. And from a spiritual perspective, what was said of Lot could be the description of every Christian believer no matter where you live. *"Lot...was a good man, sick of the terrible wickedness he saw all around him every day..."* (2 Peter 2:7 TLB).

We may not be living in Sodom, but the same cultural and spiritual dynamics at work can vex us to the point of mental angst and heart restlessness—enemies of personal health and wholeness.

At the epicenter of this malaise, the Holy Spirit holds out to you and me this magnificent promise of peace and rest that comes when Christ shepherds our lives: "He makes me lie down in green pastures."

The picture this statement paints almost seems absurd in stark contrast to the world we find ourselves in. If you're living life "at the edge" physically, emotionally, relationally, financially or spiritually right now you can almost hear yourself say, "Oh come on, get real!"

But the truth is, the "real" world is the Bible world. When the Lord shepherds my life, fear and inner conflict won't rob me of rest and peace. His personal presence is why the most timid and fragile of sheep do not need to be bound by fear which paralyzes and unrest which diminishes and debilitates.

When I come to know Him and have learned to hear His voice in His Word by the ministry of the Holy Spirit who lives in me, soul rest and peace of mind can be mine.

LEARNING TO LIE DOWN

The Hebrew word for "to lie down" is "rabats." It means to

literally stretch out and relax. Psalm 23 says the Lord *"makes"* me to lie down. It doesn't say the Lord suggests we take a break or at least slow up a bit. No, it means the Lord actually causes us to lie down. There is no other interpretation.

The Lord knows better than we do what we need. He understands without His rest and peace we will suffer the consequences of mental, physical, emotional and spiritual breakdown to some degree. Therefore He literally brings us to a place where we are made to lie down. And it is not just a time when the causes for weariness are removed. It is a place where He is present for the purpose of an encounter that truly brings renewal of mind, heart and spirit.

He knows we need the quiet, so sometimes He arranges (or permits) circumstances we would have never welcomed in the natural to take us aside and refresh us through soul-searchings in *"green pastures"* of His choosing.

"LORD, I GIVE UP!"

When David said *"The Lord makes me to lie down,"* it means the Lord leads me to a place where I finally stop striving in my own will and strength. It is where my mental, emotional and spiritual condition before Him is as though I stretch myself out in a relaxed repose. It is the picture of us in those times when we have finally done all we can to cope, or to deal with a situation or confront a circumstance in life. It is when we have ceased our restless activity and expending of energy—whether it's running from temptation, fighting a spiritual battle, trying to resolve a family issue or whatever the challenge may be.

We finally come before His presence and admit, "Lord, I just can't do this anymore!" or "Lord, now what would you have me to do?" or "Lord, please help me because I can't take another step!" or "Lord, I give up!"

We have come to the end of our solutions, ideas, attempts, plans, strategies, analogies, wisdom and our strength. It's as though the movie of our life has paused to a still frame.

The difference between those times becoming crisis that crush and destroy or the pause that refreshes and renews is whether I am willing to turn to Him in trust with all my heart and give Him the most valuable commodity I have. This commodity is time. It is moments spent in prayer, the Word and in honest and sincere communion with Him. For you see, it is nothing for God to solve the problem, provide for the need, or work the miracle. The promise of Scripture makes it clear: *"And my God will meet all your needs according to His glorious riches in Christ Jesus"* (Philippians 4:19). *"And God is able to make all grace abound to you, so that in all things at all times, having all that you need, you will abound in every good work"* (2 Corinthians 9:8).

The hard part for God is to bring us to a place where we decide to rest and find peace in His presence. And that always requires us coming to the end of ourselves in some manner.

There is absolutely no way to obtain rest and peace the Good Shepherd gives apart from time spent in fellowship with Him. And as busy as our lives are, it does seem we always have time for the things that really capture our interest and affection.

Jesus said, *"Peace I leave with you; My peace I give you. I do not give to you as the world gives. Do not let your hearts be troubled and do not be afraid"* (John 14:27). The Greek word for peace here is "eirene." It means "quietness and rest with harmony and accord"—more than the absence of strife or trouble. This conveys a tranquility which comes from a sense of security and safety even in the midst of adverse situations and unwelcome circumstances. It is also the same word that describes the peace those who have died in the Lord are presently experiencing (Romans 2:5-10). The reason it is peace is because we are in the presence of the Good Shepherd who is the Prince of Peace.

Jesus says, *"Come to Me, all you who are wearied and burdened, and I will give you rest. Take My yoke upon you and learn from Me, for I am gentle and humble in heart, and you will find rest for your souls. For My yoke is easy and My burden is light"* (Matthew 11:28).

This is the image of us when we become exhausted from carrying a burden the Lord never placed upon us. For His *"burden is light."* It is the weight of life's turns of events or the oppression from our spiritual enemy.

The Lord then offers His invitation to "yoke" ourselves with Him in personal fellowship, communion and worship. Although He does not promise to take away the burden, for that is what makes us strong, He does promise soul refreshment and strength. The Greek word for "rest" here is "anapano." It means "to cause or permit one to cease from movement or labor in order to recover and collect strength and to be refreshed." The word for "soul" is "psuche" meaning the center of our desires, emotions, will and intellect.

INNER HARMONY

Jesus' invitation to the wearied and heavy laden is a yoke of trust, surrender, fellowship and communion in order that *"He may strengthen you with power through His Spirit in your inner being"* (Ephesians.3:16).

———

A good night's sleep will refresh you physically. But it takes the Spirit of the Lord to bring rest to your soul.

The Holy Spirit brings harmony and accord within. This is harmony between our desires and our will and His desires and His will for us.

There is peace and security and a sense of rest which descends when you are at peace with the Lord. And even if the circumstances have not changed as yet, there is assurance and rest knowing you have the favor of the Lord.

We always have reason to maintain a faith-filled outlook. And we can choose to reaffirm our faith and encourage ourselves with a positive attitude, or some self-help discipline which is needful at times. But this is not what we're talking about here. For example, the Apostle Peter had more than a positive attitude going for him while in a boat in the middle of a storm when he stepped out of the vessel and walked on the water.

A FRESH ENCOUNTER

It takes more than optimism to release the miracle power of God. Peter had a focused attention upon Jesus and was responding obediently to the voice command of the Lord. In fact, there's an interesting passage in the Old Testament that reveals the false peace the people of God were conjuring for themselves just by exercising positive "self talk." *"They dress the wound of my people as though it were not serious. 'Peace, peace,' they say, when there is no peace"* (Jeremiah 8:11).

It's like standing in front of the mirror with a gunshot wound to the head, saying, "Every day and in every way I am becoming better and better." When in reality what is needed is an encounter with a crack surgeon and an emergency medical team!

There will come times when I need more than counsel from a friend or pastor, more than fellowship in a small group or Bible study, or the help any ministry program in the church can provide.

A moment arrives when only a fresh encounter with the presence of the Lord by His Spirit will give me what I need.

Jesus says if you are wearied and heavy laden, *"come to Me."* There's an hour when you and I need to hear His voice speak to us specifically and give assurance and direction—when only an obedient response to His speaking voice to our hearts will move us out of the confines of a dilemma which robs us of our joy and diminishes our life potential. Jesus said, *"My sheep listen to My voice; I know them and they follow Me"* (John 10:27).

The Lord is always leading us somewhere, not conducting a cosmic experiment with our lives. Eternity is filled with purpose. God is continually working *"in you to will and to act according to His good purpose"* (Philippians 2:13).

Whether it is a prayerful commitment, a resolute decision or some determined action, God's Word to us will always call for an obedient response. Rest and peace fills our hearts and minds only when we commit to obey.

GREAT FRUSTRATION

I recall a time when I had resigned as senior pastor of a church and there was no immediate open door. My wife and I knew our ministry effectiveness had maximized it's potential at this particular church and we felt God was directing us to prepare ourselves for the next assignment which would come from Him.

We didn't know where or when, but we knew undoubtedly we had been "brought out" of that situation by His gracious leading. We put our house up for sale in a seller's market, anticipating to realize the equity in our house within thirty to sixty days, as that was the average time most homes remained on the market. Ours was a large, attractive home next to seventy five acres of wetlands. We listed with the number one sales office in our city and our broker was a fine Christian woman. And yet our house remained on the market for nearly four months with very little interest shown, much less an offer to consider.

It was a great frustration to us as well as to our real estate agent. One morning around 4:00 A.M. I went to my study at home and began to seek the Lord. It was a time and circumstance in which the Lord was making me to lie down in prayerful communion with Him. I had come to the end of my ability to do all that was right and necessary to sell our house. So I asked the Lord if there was anything in all of this situation I had missed. Then I asked Him specifically about the price of our home.

You see, we had always just looked to the real estate agent for such detail. In response to my question, it's as though I heard the Spirit of the Lord say to me, "Thanks for asking." He impressed me with a particular price and then He spoke to my heart about changing our real estate agent and then we would be "good to go."

This was particularly difficult because she was a fine woman, an excellent agent and our listing with her had not yet expired. I didn't understand what it all meant but I shared it with my wife and we agreed to obey what I felt the Lord had spoken.

When we re-listed our house with an agent I felt the Lord direct us to, it was shown the following weekend and two offers came in. We sold the house to a couple who had been looking for over three years. Every detail of the home and property was what they had searched for and could not find.

The price was the maximum they could afford without having to sell their existing home which meant there were no contingencies in the offer. They had an adequate cash down payment, bank financing and the sale closed in forty five days.

They were acquaintances of the agent we had first listed with, and yet they had never been interested in viewing our home. It wasn't that either agent was better than the other, it was just one of those times when the Lord was "making us to lie down."

More important than looking to a real estate agent, the Good Shepherd was wanting us to hear His voice and He used this place and time to make that known in a very real way. Rest and peace came to our hearts immediately after we had taken the steps to obey what we knew was the voice of the Holy Spirit. Peace from obeying came first. The answer of a sold house arrived later.

GREEN PASTURES; GOD'S ANSWER TO OUR FEARS

Another wonderful result the Good Shepherd achieves in making us *"lie down in green pastures"* is that fear departs from our lives. Later we will talk about the *"valley of the shadow of death"* and the strength to *"fear no evil."* But I don't feel it is in the *"valley of the shadow of death"* God deals with our fears. It is in the "green pastures."

––––––––––––––– ⚙ –––––––––––––––

I don't believe the Lord drives fear out of our lives by placing us in fearful places. This happens in the "green pasture" where we learn to love and trust Him and fear is driven from our lives.

Fear must be dealt with and the walk of faith strengthened by the Word of the Lord to our hearts if we are going to be able to walk fearlessly through *"the valley of the shadow of death."*

I don't reassure a fearful child by putting on a scary mask and confronting him in the dark. I nourish the confidence of a fearful youngster through love, truth and the strength of a trusting relationship.

When you trust and reverence the Lord, then all other fear which seeks to control and dominate will lose its paralyzing grip. That's what *"lying down in green pastures"* is all about.

Sheep won't lay down when they are fearful. The fact that Psalm 23 says the Lord *"makes me to lie down"* infers He deals with the dominating fears of my life.

A PHOBIA-FILLED WORLD

People today are consumed with fear. The number of phobias which have been identified by psychologists today is absolutely astounding. Here are just a few:

Fear of the color purple—*porphyrophobia.*
Fear of the color yellow—*xanthophobia.*
Fear of seeing yourself in the mirror—*eisoptrophobia.*
Fear of sleep—*somniphobia.*
Fear of being touched—*aphenphosmphobia.*
Fear of small things—*microphobia.*
Fear of accidents—*dystychiphobia.*
Fear of gravity—*barophobia.*
Fear of flowers—*anthrophobia.*
Fear of hair—*hypertricherophobia.*
Fear of going bald—*phalacrophobia.*
Fear of paper—*papyrophobia.*
Fear of church—*ecclesiophobia.*
Fear of air—*anemophobia.*
Fear of going to bed—*clinophobia.*
Fear of clouds—*nephobia.*
Fear of light—*photophobia.*
Fear of trees—*dendrophobia.*
Fear of freedom—*eleutherophobia.*
Fear of hell—*hadephobia.*
Fear of #8—*octophobia.*
Fear of #13—*triskadekaphobia.*

Fear of everybody—*sociophobia*.
Fear of everything—*panophobia*.

Medical and mental health professionals recognize the problem. It is estimated that 13% of all people suffer from some kind of anxiety without finding effective cures. Thousands with more serious social anxiety problems are put on medications that warn of side effects.

I came across a medication being advertised which promised to relieve anxiety fast and gave statistics that promoted its success rate among those with occasional anxiety to those who suffer with phobias. The website for the medication also listed the possible side effects. They include: drowsiness, fatigue, stomach upset, headache, restlessness, morning grogginess, increasing the effects of sedative drugs, and lowering of blood pressure. To put it bluntly, I guess you could say it works by making you too sick to care about anything else!

Another solution is promoted as a proven method to free yourself from anxiety. It's advertising promises to be the most powerful and private subliminal therapy to change your life. Claiming the key to freedom from social anxiety is in the subconscious mind, the promise being that self-hypnosis, subliminal audio CD's are guaranteed to supercharge your social life.

More than all of these, Christian counseling can certainly help by pinpointing the source of such fears. But we should never fail to prescribe a course of action that combines faith in God's love, grace and power, a correct view of ourselves in light of the Word of God, as well as a support structure of caring friends.

"THE SPIRIT OF FEAR"

Our fears can only be mastered when we see ourselves in light of our relationship to God who is always the greater "fact" no matter how large or legitimate our fears may loom.

The Bible calls Satan the *"god of this world"* who has blinded the minds of those who don't believe the Gospel (2 Corinthians 4:4). Satan rules his kingdom on earth through fear and intimidation. Control by fear is the essence of witchcraft. This fallen world rotates on its axis in an environment of fear and anxiety.

Jesus said it would become so intense that men's hearts would fail them because of fear's influence, in expectation of those things which are coming upon the earth (Luke 21:26).

Even the Christian believer feels the oppression of such a fearful atmosphere. Although most anxiety is an emotional response to danger, either real or imagined, there is a condition the Bible calls *"the spirit of fear"* (2 Timothy 1:7). "Spirit" (pneuma/Greek) means "the vital principle by which the physical body is animated, or given life." It also means "a spirit being; angelic or demonic."

It is my belief that in the spirit realm there are forces at work to oppress with abnormal fear and to undermine trust in God. They are literally *spirits* of fear. David said the fear which rules this world is man-made, and results from not trusting God. It also brings bondage and enslavement. *"Fear of man will prove to be a snare, but whoever trusts in the Lord is kept safe"* (Proverbs 29:25).

The Bible says there's a fear that isn't from the Lord—and it brings torment. The antidote to this condition is to know the love of God. *"There is no fear in love; but perfect love casts out fear, because fear involves torment. But he who fears has not been made perfect in love. We love Him because He first loved us"* (1 John 4:18-19 NKJV).

We may not love God perfectly, but His perfect love for us is what casts out fear.

It is these kinds of fear the Good Shepherd wants to drive from our lives and does so by making us to *"lie down in green pastures."*

GREEN PASTURES; THE PLACE OF HABITATION WITH GOD

"Green pastures" is the Hebrew word "na'ah"—"a place of habitation, a home, a pleasant land filled with new grass, young herbs or fresh vegetation."

In our "encounter times" in the presence of the Lord there will always be a fresh revelation of the person of Jesus Christ to our minds and hearts. It is never a dry, desert or undesirable location. Rather, it is place of "habitation" which means God is showing us it is only in His presence we can best live, prosper and succeed. It is a new understanding that our real home and habitation is in the presence of the Lord.

We were created to be with Him. *"Green pastures"* is descriptive of soul nourishment which is fresh and new.

The Holy Spirit never speaks in clichés and platitudes. I have found that the voice of the Good Shepherd speaks in terms which are clearly understandable to my own mind and way of thinking. He may not speak in agreement with my thoughts, but His voice is so personal He gets my attention because He often speaks in His very familiar language.

When I had sought the Lord concerning the sale of our house and He spoke to my heart and gave direction, I also heard the promise of answered prayer in the words, *"and you'll be good to go"*—in terms familiar to me. I don't ever remember the Lord's voice speaking to my heart using the King James English. Even though I study out of the King James version of the Scriptures, His personal thoughts to me have never contained a *"yea verily"* or a *"most assuredly I say unto thee!"*

My Dilemma

To further illustrate the freshness of the Spirit's voice, there was an instance when I was in the throws of a major decision concerning the future of pastoral ministry of a particular congregation. I met with the church board who had finally decided to take the side of what I would refer to as a few "power brokers" in the membership. Feeling threatened and fearful from their opposition to the ministry there, the board had also lent a sympathetic ear to a disloyal staff member with his own agenda serving as the liaison between the disgruntled in the church and the church board.

In my estimation, they made this choice rather than embrace a clearly stated, God-given and faith-challenging vision and mission for the church. Such a vision obviously required them to also stand in support of the pastoral leadership which they declined to do.

My story is not unique. To my amazement, in conversations with friends and others I was made aware how often this scenario is repeated in "politically correct" but "Kingdom incorrect" churches across the country.

In that moment I needed to decide whether I was going to press what I knew was God's directive for ministry for that particular church—which was the destiny God had prepared for them in their city. *"For we are God's workmanship, created in Christ Jesus to do good works, which God prepared in advance for us to do"* (Ephesians 2:10). Or I had to decide to step aside and allow the Lord to be the master of my own destiny and leave His church to Him.

A PLACE OF REST

In those times of inner deliberation I heard the Lord speak so clearly to my heart saying, *"Take your hands off, because I have."* He didn't say *"My son, my son I say unto thee in this thine hour of challenge."* No, He said, *"Take your hands off!"* In an instant, I understood precisely what the Lord was saying.

―――――――― ⌐✻✻✻✻⌐ ――――――――

I saw in my spirit what the eventual outcome of the situation would be.

As I obeyed, during the following months my wife and I were ushered into what can only be described as a *"green pasture."* It was a place of mental and physical rest, fellowship with the Lord, renewal in our relationship with one another that the demands of full-time ministry have a way of stealing from you, a revival of prayer together, a period of fresh consecration to true "Kingdom work," a reconfirming of who we were in ministry and what we had been called to be and to do as a husband-and-wife leadership team in Christ's Kingdom work.

It was an oasis of God's wonderful provision for us in every way—spiritually, financially, emotionally and socially. Now that's what I call a "green pasture."

We made the wonderful discovery of what true friendships in the Lord really looked like during that time. It was all the Hebrew word "na'ah" for green pastures means—"a habitation, a home, a pleasant place filled with new grass and fresh vegetation."

Rest—A Work of the Spirit

Every time the Lord brings you to the end of yourself, the death of a vision, an unwelcome situation or adverse circumstances which stop you dead in the tracks your busy life has been making, He has really brought you to a *"green pasture"* of encounter with Him—a place of peace and rest.

When David wrote, "He makes me to lie down in green pastures," it parallels the poetic description of His own experience as expressed in Psalm 4.

Probably the lowest time in David's journey was when he was fleeing for his life from his own son. Absalom had led a rebellion against his father, usurped control of the kingdom and was attempting to kill David. Psalm 4 was written during this flight from Absalom and in the face of being heartlessly forsaken by his people for another king.

David worships during this dark time and expresses his praise in song. *"You have put gladness in my heart, More than when their grain and new wine abound. In peace I will both lie down and sleep, For You alone, O LORD, make me to dwell in safety"* (Psalm 4:7-8 RSV).

The Spirit of the Lord filled his heart with rest and peace in a greater way than when he experienced times of the outward evidence of God's blessing. It was as much a work of the Holy Spirit as it is in us today.

God wants you to experience Spirit-imparted rest and peace no matter what your circumstances may be. The Lord has not changed. If He would do that for David under the Old Covenant, how much more should you and I under the New Covenant blessings of Jesus, our Prince of Peace, be assured He will encounter you and me in the same marvelous way.

CHAPTER FIVE

FINDING HIS WAYS
ARE PERFECT

"He leads me beside still waters."
−PSALM 23:2 NKJV

It is interesting that sheep will rarely drink from a fast-moving stream. They are better fit in nature and disposition for drinking from quiet or still pools of water.

"He leads me beside still waters" is the picture of the shepherd providing for the sheep in a way He knows is best for them. When the Lord shepherds my life His methods are always exactly right for me. The patterns and people He uses, the situations He directs and the schemata He masterminds in working His will are always in harmony with the good outcome and blessed destination He has determined.

The Lord accomplishes this work in me by the ministry of His Holy Spirit whom Jesus said would come after He ascended to heaven (John 16:7). It is always a final result designed to bring to me His best blessing, and to bring to Him the greatest glory.

I used to have a decal pasted to an electric keyboard I played when I was a church staff music director. It served as a constant reminder that the music presentation would only be personally rewarding when it truly touched the souls and spirits of people. And it would only touch lives when it was done in worship to the Lord, not as a showpiece for talent. The decal stated: "When the Master is glorified, the servant is satisfied."

This reminded me that true joy is found not only in doing things with excellence in an entertaining style, but also God's way and for His honor in a Holy Spirit-empowered manner.

A PERFECT PLAN

When the Lord shepherds your life, one aspect of what He is doing is to show you His ways are perfect. Scripture declares, *"As for God, His way is perfect"* (2 Samuel 22:31 NKJV). The word *"way"* (derek/Hebrew) means "the course of life." And the word *"perfect"* (tamiym) is translated, "what is complete and entirely in harmony with truth and fact."

When David said the Lord *"leads me beside still waters,"* the Holy Spirit is communicating to us that when the Lord shepherds our lives He will move us along a track entirely in harmony with the truth of God's Word. David writes, *"Your Word is a lamp for my feet and a light for my path"* (Psalm 119:105 NLT).

_____

The Bible has an answer for every question in life, either directly or in principle.

All along our course we will find His provision and blessing custom-tailored to meet our every need as we make the Word of God the lamp for our feet and the light for our path.

God knows you intimately and completely. Psalm 139 says you were not only a twinkle in your parents' eyes, but before your first cry outside of the womb you were a person upon whom God's heart desired to lavish His love and blessing. You were one for whom God was committed to fulfill His wonderful plans.

No matter the circumstances surrounding your birth, there is no such thing as a biological accident to God. With Him, every child is a "planned and wanted child." *"I praise You because I am fearfully and wonderfully made; Your works are wonderful, I know that full well. My frame was not hidden from You when I was made in the secret place. When I was woven together in the depths of the earth,*

Your eyes saw my unformed body. All the days ordained for me were written in Your book before one of them came to be. How precious to me are Your thoughts, O God! How vast is the sum of them!" (Psalm 139:14-17).

No matter where you go or what you do, God never changes His mind about you or His plan for your future. Life is God's starting point with you and salvation through faith in Jesus Christ is your starting point with God. Life is God's gift to you; what you do with it is your gift to God.

THE LORD ALWAYS USES HIS PEOPLE

A conversation I had with a close friend and relative illustrates the truth that from the beginning God never changes His mind concerning His children.

While at lunch one day my friend, who at one time attended church and actively served the Lord but in recent years had not been doing so, questioned me about an incident he had experienced. Years previously, while busy in the church and involved in a teaching ministry, God had given him faith to believe for a healing touch in the life of a young man who had been seriously injured in a football game.

Just an hour or so before surgery which had been scheduled to remove an injured kidney, my friend spoke with the young man's father and urged him to have one last check to see if the operation was really necessary. He had a strong belief God had miraculously touched this young man in a healing way in answer to his prayer.

Reluctantly, the father did so—and to their amazement, the kidney was restored to health and surgery was not needed.

Now years later, although he made no profession of faith in quite the same way today as he had years previously, he had been strongly prompted to call a friend with whom he had no contact for a long time. When he placed the call, he told the individual she had been on his mind and he just needed to call. Surprised, she told him how she had just lost her best friend in death and would have given anything to talk with him but didn't know how he could be reached.

His question to me was, "Is that just coincidence, the power of the human mind, or what?"

My best answer for him was that I believed it illustrated two things.

First, God loved the individual who was grieving over the loss of a friend and He knew he was the one to encourage and comfort her like no one else really could in her time of sorrow.

Second, just as he had compassion for the hurting and faith in God to meet human need in the past, it was a statement to him that after all these years God had not changed His mind about how He wanted to use him, bless him and make him a blessing to others.

GOD HAS PLANS FOR YOU

Eternal God, who is beyond time and space, sees at once the beginning and the end of our lives and all the days in between. He views the final outcome He has so marvelously and superbly planned for us.

The book of Jude gives us this wonderful promise with respect to both God's ability and desire for you and me. *"To Him who is able to keep you from falling and to present you before His glorious presence without fault and with great joy"* (Jude 24).

God makes this very personal statement of care and blessing. *"'For I know the plans I have for you,' declares the LORD, 'plans to prosper you and not to harm you, plans to give you hope and a future'"* (Jeremiah 29:11).

Yet, being creatures of time and space and not seeing the beginning from the end, we are called to a walk of obedient faith assured by the promises of God. *"However, as it is written: 'No eye has seen, no ear has heard, no mind has conceived what God has prepared for those who love Him', but God has revealed it to us by his Spirit"* (1 Corinthians 2:9-10).

Our journey of faith in fellowship with Him through the indwelling Holy Spirit is meant to be a lifelong revelation revealing His ways are perfect. For He also understands us infinitely well enough to know what means and methods to take us into the tomorrows which are our destiny in Him.

THE HOLY SPIRIT'S SUPPLY

David didn't say the Good Shepherd leads me *"to"* still waters. He said God leads me *"beside"* still waters. It declares that no matter where the Lord leads us, all along the pathway there are *"still waters."* Each new discovery is an awe-inspiring realization of the presence and power of the Holy Spirit.

When in the throws of making a decision that would change the direction of my future, and anxious to know the will of the Lord concerning it, I received one of the best pieces of reassuring counsel from a pastor who is now with the Lord. He simply stated, "When you need to know, you'll know."

It was true. Three weeks later when I needed to know, I had the answer from the Lord to make the right decision. A wonderful promise given by God along these same lines is found in Deuteronomy 33:25: *"Your strength will equal your days."*

The pathway of our obedient faith, embracing His destiny is the discovery that all along the way His provision for us is just exactly what we need in the manner and time we need it.

God never calls us to a life that we can live.
He calls us to a life that He lives in and through us.

"Still waters" represent the provision of the Holy Spirit.

THE SPIRIT WILL FLOW

Since throughout Scripture water serves as a type or picture of the Holy Spirit, I believe this analogy can be applied here without doing exegetical injustice to the text. The ways of God are the ways of His Spirit's leading and working. Our best attempts at living for God and following His leading will be a failure without the power of the Holy Spirit.

Sin's impact has made our flesh impotent to do the will of God. This enabling flows from the Holy Spirit who lives within us. The

TERRY KIRSCHMAN

Lord assures the refreshment and blessing of His Spirit to every thirsty soul. *"For I will pour water on him who is thirsty, and floods on the dry ground; I will pour My Spirit on your descendants, And My blessing on your offspring"* (Isaiah 44:3 NKJV).

God promises, *"And I will put my Spirit in you and move you to follow My decrees and be careful to keep My laws"* (Ezekiel 36:27). It is also the promise of Jesus. *"'Whoever believes in Me, as the Scripture has said, streams of living water will flow from within him.' By this He meant the Spirit, whom those who believed in Him were later to receive. Up to that time the Spirit had not been given, since Jesus had not yet been glorified"* (John 7:38-39).

Paul writes, *"So I say, live by the Spirit and you will not gratify the desires of the sinful nature...Since we live by the Spirit let us keep in step with the Spirit"* (Galatians 5:16,25).

THE WORD "PENETRATES"

There is nothing more tragic than a misspent life. We all know of individuals or have read of people who never rose to their full potential. Life lived without the Holy Spirit's empowering is a misspent life no matter how noteworthy to society, because there is more to our existence than what we experience on earth. God's design is for us to make an eternal impact, one that has influence beyond the grave.

Spirit-empowered prayers live on long after the ones who prayed them.

The ways of God for the *glory* of God are the ways of His Spirit. The Almighty's provision and enabling always accompanies His leading. The provisional power of the Lord for my life is found as I understand and yield to the ministry of the Holy Spirit.

The ability to read and understand the Bible as the Father's message to you personally is dependent upon your relationship with the Holy Spirit. *"For the word of God is living and active, sharper than any double-edged sword, it penetrates even to dividing soul and spirit, joints and marrow; it judges the thoughts and attitudes of the heart"* (Hebrews 4:12). *"The man without the Spirit does not accept the things that come from the Spirit of God, for they are foolishness to him, and he cannot understand them, because they are spiritually discerned"* (1 Corinthians 2:14).

The character likeness of Jesus is the ultimate goal of God the Father for every believer. *"For those God foreknew He also predestined to be conformed to the likeness of His Son..."* (Romans 8:29). These character traits are described as the *"fruit of the Spirit"* in Galatians 5:22 (love, joy, peace, patience, kindness, goodness, faithfulness, gentleness, self-control).

The calling and equipping for service and ministry in the church are gifts of grace (charisma/Greek) from the Spirit and are listed in Romans 12:6-8 including; exhorting, serving, teaching, encouraging, generous giving, leading and showing mercy.

The supernatural gifts of the Holy Spirit which transcend our human ability to minister to others are listed in 1 Corinthians 12:1-11. They include gifts of power, gifts of revelation, and gifts of utterance. I suggest that more than anything else, it is beside the *"still waters"* of the Holy Spirit's resources of enabling and empowerment (dunamis/Greek) that the Good Shepherd leads us to drink deeply time and time again.

It is worth noting once more how He leads us continually beside *"still waters"*—never *to* or *away* from. This detail is not insignificant; it is profoundly important. And the Holy Spirit recorded it through David's writing in those exact terms. The old adage, "You can lead one to water but you can't make one drink" also applies to the ministry of the Holy Spirit in our lives. We have as much of the Holy Spirit's presence and power as we are thirsty for.

QUENCHING OUR THIRST FOR SPIRITUAL EXPERIENCE

As was stated earlier, leading the sheep *"beside still waters"* is a picture of the Good Shepherd providing for the flock in a way He knows they are fit to receive.

In creation God gave us a human spirit which is receptive to impressions from the spiritual realm. By nature our human spirit cries out to experience more than what our physical, emotional, and intellectual nature can know through the five senses. It longs for a supernatural encounter.

In the superfluity of religions in the world today, the metaphysical and paranormal have become the subject of scientific study as well as the topic of Hollywood productions. The supernatural is prevalent on the motion picture screen. Biblical themes of spiritual warfare, apocalypse and ancient prophetic writings are a hit in movies and books. The reason is because it appeals to the spiritual nature of man.

However:

- The best Hollywood can offer the human spirit is entertainment and fantasy.
- The best religion can offer the human spirit is superstition and legalism.
- The best science can offer the human spirit is to explain the supernatural in terms of force fields and electrical impulses.
- The best mysticism can offer the human spirit is encounters with counterfeit spirits of darkness seeking to control by deception, fear, oppression and ultimately possession.

In regeneration, our human spirit becomes fit to receive the presence and ministry of the Holy Spirit because through faith and repentance the blood of Jesus has cleansed the human temple of resident sin, guiltiness, and is now fit for the Holy Spirit's habitation.

Our human spirit's longing for a supernatural encounter with the one true God is met when we receive the Spirit of Christ. It is our human spirit that comes alive to God at salvation and communes with the Spirit of God. Jesus said, *"No one can see the kingdom of God unless he is born again...Flesh gives birth to flesh. But Spirit gives birth to spirit"* (John 3:3,6).

So unless we are born again by the Spirit of God we cannot know the truth concerning the spiritual reality of His kingdom nor enter into the life of that kingdom. By the grace of God through faith in Christ the Holy Spirit has taken up residence in and brought life to the human spirit. In fact, Scripture declares that one of the identifying characteristics of born again Christian believers is for them to be influenced and directed by the Holy Spirit. *"For as many as are led by the Spirit of God, these are sons of God"* (Romans 8:14 NKJV).

REFRESHINGS NEVER CEASE

When the Good Shepherd leads us "beside still waters," He is guiding us to the source of our spiritual strength and empowerment.

The Lord is bringing us to ongoing infillings, refreshings and encounters with the ministry of the Holy Spirit.

This is what the apostle Paul said was the will of God for us, about which we should be fully aware. *"Therefore do not be unwise, but understand what the will of the Lord is. And do not be drunk with wine, in which is dissipation; but be filled with the Spirit, speaking to one another in psalms and hymns and spiritual songs, singing and making melody in your heart to the Lord, giving thanks always for all things to God the Father in the name of our Lord Jesus Christ, submitting to one another in the fear of God"* (Ephesians 5:17-21 NKJV).

The verb *"filled"* (pleroo/Greek) is present perfect tense. It means a continual filling.

THE IMPERATIVE OF RIGHT RELATIONSHIPS

A humorous story is told about a man who went forward for prayer in a service, asking the Lord to fill him with the Spirit. His wife, from her seat in the back of the church, prayed out loud for others to hear, "Don't do it Lord, he leaks!"

This humorous apologue illustrates two things. First we do leak! There is a drain of moral and spiritual strength in our beings when we resist (Acts 7:51), quench (1 Thessalonians.5:19), or grieve (Ephesians 4:30) the Holy Spirit's ministry in our life. To our own detriment, all of us are guilty.

There is also a need for refreshings and empowering encounters in prayerful fellowship with the Holy Spirit in order to face the spiritual and moral challenges a fallen world confronts us with every day. It was the experience of the church of Acts and it is for the church now (Acts 4:1-31).

Second, it points out the error of perceiving the continual infillings of the Holy Spirit only as spiritual events with certain corresponding manifestations, rather than a relationship outcome. The result of a vital walk with the Lord in communion with the Holy Spirit will be ongoing infillings and enablings by the ministry of the Holy Spirit in us. Notice in Ephesians 5:17-21 that being *"filled with the Spirit"* is synonymous with the strengthening of right relationships.

Our fellowship with the Lord is enhanced—the result being a renewed song of praise and a thankful heart. Our relationships with one another are strengthened, the outcome being spiritual ministry to each other and a caring attitude of humility and submission. In fact, all of the gifts of the Spirit function only in the environment of right relationships with God and one another.

If our associations are not right, we may be led beside *"still waters"* of the Holy Spirit's supply, but we will not drink. The demonstration of spiritual gifts, whether they be gifts of leadership (Ephesians 4:11-12, 1 Timothy 3:1-13), gifts of ministry (Romans 12:3-12) or supernatural gifts of power, revelation and utterance (1 Corinthians12:4-11), may digress from disorderly conduct at best to carnal demonstrations of spiritual abuse at worst, when relationships with God and one another are not how they should be.

An Unlimited Supply

For God to place the gifts of His Spirit in the lives of those who are not committed to right relationships would be like putting weapons of mass destruction in the hands of spiritual terrorists. All of the gifts the Holy Spirit imparts are for the transformation and edification of the spiritual and moral lives of God's people, to conform us to the likeness of Jesus and for the strengthening of the corporate life and ministry of the church in order that we might embrace the will of God and be empowered to fulfill His vision.

"He leads me beside still waters." Those waters run cool and deep. There is an unlimited supply of the Spirit's presence and power. Your spirit has been made alive to the Holy Spirit through the miracle of new birth. He has come to minister to you in ways you are fit to receive.

Will you make it your habit to drink regularly so that Hebrews 13:20-21 can be the narrative of your life in His sheepfold? *"May the God of peace, who through the blood of the eternal covenant brought back from the dead our Lord Jesus, that great Shepherd of the sheep, equip you with everything good for doing His will, and may He work in us what is pleasing to Him, through Jesus Christ, to whom be glory for ever and ever. Amen."*

CHAPTER SIX

FINDING
SOUL RESTORATION

"He restores my soul."
– PSALM 23:3

While watching television, I observed several pharmaceutical company advertisements exhibiting their latest drug as an answer to various human maladies.

Usually I just "glaze over" during commercials or surf the wave of mindless distractions the satellite dish programming affords. But this time my attention had been captured because there were at least three of these same drug company promotionals in a row. The last one peaked my curiosity because I had never seen a drug advertised before which promised such a similar panacea and sounded so familiar to the pitch that the illicit drugs pushed to my generation in the sixties and seventies did.

This particular advertisement held my attention because the appealing audio message and the slick visuals made the promise to restore mental, emotional and physical "pep" to anyone whose busy lifestyle and demanding schedule had left them drained. The sales pitch closed with asking us to buy the drug, "Because life takes energy." Because life takes energy!?

Then I thought about what this advertisement was really saying. This "designer" drug is for all those who can't deal with the painful discovery that one of the costs of living is the energy it takes to function as a living, breathing creature. Or worse, never mind

71

reassessing your lifestyle choices in light of your physical and emotional limitations, just find a stimulant that can take you wherever it is you want to go.

Then I thought, although the packaging may have changed we have not come all that far from the drug counter-culture of the sixties after all, when "Crosby, Stills, Nash and Young" were harmonizing about "getting back to the garden." Because now, as then, the human soul becomes anemic and faint from the effects of misplaced priorities, disappointingly defective values, sinning and being sinned against.

The issue has always been to find some help to cope or something to somehow medicate the pain. And back then, a whole generation accepted the remedy so artfully celebrated in song by the most popular British band of all time as they crooned, "I get by with a little help from my friends. I get high with a little help from friends."

Today the problems really haven't changed that much. In fact, much of the same remedy offered then is now legal!

OUR GOD-GIVEN NATURE

Made in the image of God, we are triune in nature. We are a spirit and soul in a body.

The spirit is the part of our nature which is sensitive to the spirit realm, but it is dead in relationship with God. At salvation, it is our spirit which comes alive to God as the Holy Spirit takes up residence within us. *"And you He made alive, who were dead in trespasses and sins, in which you once walked according to the course of this world, according to the prince of the power of the air, the spirit who now works in the sons of disobedience"* (Ephesians 2:1-2 NKJV). *"...your body is the temple of the Holy Spirit..."* (1Corinthians 6:19 NKJV).

It is to our spirit the Holy Spirit communicates with—and it is the human spirit united with the soul that will live forever. For the Christian believer it will be housed in a new glorified body like the Lord's resurrected body. For the unbeliever the spirit and soul will be banished from the presence of God, living consciously in hell.

In Hebrew, the term *"soul"* (nephesh) means "our vitality as a living being; the core of our emotions, passions and appetites; the center of activity for our mind and will; the defining aspects of our character."

It is this facet of our being that is so damaged by sin. Because of the Fall of man, our mind cannot understand the things of God, our heart cannot love unconditionally and our will cannot do the will of God. It is our selfish desires which motivate us.

The *"mystery of iniquity"* (2 Thessalonians 2:7) is indeed the incomprehendable depths of sin's perverse impact upon the human soul. To reverse this condition it takes "soul restoration"— the work of God's Spirit and the Word, with our cooperation. New Birth enlivens our spirit to the Holy Spirit and relationship and fellowship with God are established.

The blood of Christ has covered our sin and removed even the *record* of our iniquity against God. *"Having wiped out the handwriting of requirements that was against us, which was contrary to us. And He has taken it out of the way, having nailed it to the cross"* (Colossians 2:13-14 NKJV).

We are forgiven and have a right "position" before God. But the restoration of the "condition" of our souls is a work of the Word and the Spirit which will take the rest of our lives.

Just as we made a decision to respond to God's initiative to convict and to save us, and we repented and believed, so we must make ongoing decisions in life about how we will cooperate with the Lord's restoring work in our soul. We can cooperate, or we can remain in a justified "position" before the Lord but never improve our spiritual "condition" in Him.

SOUL RESTORATION AND THE SANCTIFIED LIFE

The Holy Spirit prompted David to use the word *"restore"* when He spoke of the Lord's influence upon the human soul. *"Restore"* (shuwb/Hebrew) means several things, including: "to cause or allow to return; to relinquish; to be refreshed; to be repaired." It is most often

73

used in the context figuratively of spiritual and human relationships.

In comparison, the term *"sanctify"* (quadash/Hebrew) means "to make oneself ceremonially clean; to prepare; to dedicate; to be separate." The New Testament term *"sanctify"* (hagiazo/Greek) similarly is "to separate from things profane and dedicate to God."

When you received Christ's forgiveness by faith and were born again by the Holy Spirit, you received a new disposition, inclination or ability to make such a decision to be set apart. Your spirit has come alive to the ministry of the Holy Spirit, and your sinful nature is not annihilated, but subdued.

To cultivate a lifestyle which lives in the strength and in accordance with the principles of this new nature is the lifelong challenge we all face as long as we are alive in this body. It is what the apostle Paul confessed. *"I do not understand what I do. For what I want to do I do not do, but what I hate I do. And if I do what I do not want to do, I agree that the law is good. As it is, it is no longer I myself who do it, but it is sin living in me. I know that nothing good lives in me, that is, in my sinful nature. For I have the desire to do what is good, but I cannot carry it out. For what I do is not the good I want to do; no, the evil I do not want to do—this I keep on doing. Now if I do what I do not want to do, it is no longer I who do it, but it is sin living in me that does it. So I find this law at work: When I want to do good, evil is right there with me. For in my inner being I delight in God's law; but I see another law at work in the members of my body, waging war against the law of my mind and making me a prisoner* of the *law of sin at work within my members. What a wretched man I am! Who will rescue me from this body of death? Thanks be to God-through Jesus Christ our Lord!"* (Romans 7:15-25).

"IN PROCESS"

Having been raised in a pastor's home and being in the church and around believers all of my life, it has been intriguing to see this struggle demonstrated in the attitudes and actions of God's people decade after decade.

The church-going crowd has been my environment 100% of my

life. Even though I grew up learning to love the people of God and the Body of Christ, it didn't shield me from the reality that sanctification is most definitely a life-long process. And while I have spent nearly thirty years in pastoral ministry and knowing all of us as God's people are works of grace "in process," I have always been somewhat taken back by the remarkable difference in character and disposition of Christian believers. Especially when age has not been the determining factor.

In churches I have pastored I have seen the likeness of Jesus demonstrated early in the lives of new Christian believers that brings a wonder to your mind and heart and a sense of worship to your spirit for the reality of the miracle of life change. On the other hand I have witnessed "saints" who have spent years in the church exhibit behavior which betrays the leanness of their souls and their ignorance of the ways of Christ that leaves you dumfounded.

HE TOOK IT PERSONALLY!

As a senior pastor, I have made it a habit from time to time to purchase for the deacon board a book that I read and felt would be beneficial for them to read as well. It has helped to stimulate thinking on certain spiritual truths, reinforce God-given vision for the church and at least assist as a relationship encourager and faith builder. In one church I pastored, a retired Pentecostal minister also served on the deacon board and taught an adult Sunday School class. This gentleman had worked as a senior pastor in a number of churches for many years. I gave one such book to the board entitled "The Next Move of God" by Fucia Pickett.

In her book she describes certain spiritual forces at work in the church which hinder the work of God in the context of what she believes God is desiring to do in His church by the Holy Spirit. These spiritual forces are identified by the names of certain Biblical characters they influenced—including Jezebel, the Pharisees, Absalom and others.

This particular minister/board member became so angered by the description of these spirit personalities that, believe it or not, he took it personally! He proceeded to launch into a "spiritual" tirade in front of his Sunday School class and use the occasion to discredit the book as well as to publicly resign from the board.

When the Christian Education Director confronted him in the church foyer that morning about what he had done, she too became the recipient of a verbal barrage. Needless to say, his resignation from the board was accepted.

———————— ⚜ ————————

Peter states one of the evidences of sanctification is the kind of love we demonstrate toward one another as members of the body of Christ.

Again, sanctification is an outcome of our relationship with the Lord and it is demonstrated in our relationships with others. *"Since you have purified your souls in obeying the truth through the Spirit in sincere love of the brethren, love one another fervently with a pure heart"* (1 Peter 1:22 NKJV).

A FAMILY TRAGEDY

By way of contrast, in a church where I was on staff as youth pastor, a bright, extremely handsome high school graduate was invited to our church by one of the young people and became a born-again Christian. To my knowledge, Craig had little or no church background and soon I discovered he had come from a broken home.

Along with his siblings, he experienced the economic hardship, emotional devastation and the absence of a father that comes with divorce. But no one in the family took it harder than this young man's mother. Her way of dealing with the heartbreak was suicide. Her attempt however was a failure and it left her an invalid, physically scarred and mentally impaired from a self-inflicted gunshot wound to the head.

Craig's new life in Christ demonstrated through acts of love, forgiveness, kindness, grace and faith were a constant marvel to me. With all the rights in the natural to be caustically bitter and deeply resentful, the love he lavished upon his mother was obviously motivated by far more than pity. It was a genuine unconditional love which came from the divine release of forgiveness through his life for his mother for having performed the ultimately selfish act—of forsaking your children by taking your own life.

While Craig's siblings would have little to do with their mother, he would visit her weekly, keeping her up to date with the events of his life. He would wash her feet, cut her toenails, fix her hair, feed her and spend enough time to be the only one who could identify her words and understand the unique language that sputtered forth from a severely disfigured face.

On nice days, he would bundle her up, carry her out of the nursing home, place her in his little convertible and take her for a ride in the beautiful outdoors that otherwise she could only see through her window. Regardless of how she appeared to others, he loved her and was proud to be her son. He never had to be taught this in a discipleship class. It manifested as the outpouring of the "Christ life" and the evidence of the soul restoration that comes when the Lord shepherds your life.

A SURPRISING OUTCOME

It was little surprise when one day Craig shared with me how he felt that maybe the Lord was calling him to full time ministry. The problem was he had no money for college and no resources to turn to. Without asking me for help he simply shared his need and requested we pray together and believe for the Lord to provide.

Such faith in God rivaled even my own. Funds poured in from sources that even surprised Craig. Someone provided him with a more trustworthy car to go to college and he completed four years of study debt free.

Shortly before she passed away, the love, grace and forgiveness of Christ which Craig's mother saw in her son won her heart and he had the joy of leading her to the Lord. Today he is fulfilling God's call upon His life, ministering with the power and grace that brought a redemptive miracle to his mother, as he serves as the associate pastor with his father-in-law in one of the truly great churches in America.

The differences between these examples have nothing to do with the Christian believer's position in Christ. I contend that it has everything to do with a Christian believer's condition in Christ as it relates to soul restoration. Again I assert that we can be in Christ and yet the Lord not be allowed to shepherd our life. When He shepherds my life He "restores my soul."

IN TRUTH AND HOLINESS

Paul prayed, *"May God Himself, the God of peace, sanctify you through and through. May your whole spirit, soul and body be kept blameless at the coming of our Lord Jesus Christ"* (1 Thessalonians 5:23).

David wrote, *"The Law of the Lord is perfect, converting the soul..."* (Psalm19:7 NKJV). Jesus prayed, *"Make them pure and holy (sanctify) through teaching them Your words of truth...and I consecrate Myself to meet their need for growth in truth and holiness"* (John 17:17,19 TLB).

In Jesus' final prayer for the disciples, He uses the term *"sanctify"* in the context of being made clean by internal reformation of the soul. In other words, as the disciples would submit themselves to His Word, Christ's personal commitment to them was to meet their need of soul reformation and sanctification by the ministry of His Spirit, present with them and in them (John 14:17).

Here sanctification is the outcome of a right relationship with Jesus as much or more than it is just the discipline of a Bible reading program, or church-going routine. Jesus said, *"Why do you call Me 'Lord, Lord' and do not do what I say?"* (Luke 6:46).

―――――――――― ∘❦∘ ――――――――――

Just as soul restoration is presented in the context of human and spiritual relationships, so is sanctification the outcome of a right relationship with the Lord.

It is not so much the disciplined task of doing the things which make us a better Christian so that the Holy Spirit will keep His end of the bargain and clean us up, as much as it is the result of a loving committed relationship with the Good Shepherd whose likeness we emulate more and more because He is the object of our love, devotion and worship.

LEGALISM: THE PRIDE OF BEING SANCTIFIED

Without this understanding of soul restoration and sanctification, we can bear a very uncomfortable resemblance to the Pharisee in church whom Jesus spoke about when He said, *"Two men went up to the temple to pray, one a Pharisee and the other a tax collector. The Pharisee stood up and prayed about himself: 'God, I thank you that I am not like other men - robbers, evildoers, adulterers—or even like this tax collector. I fast twice a week and give a tenth of all I get.' But the tax collector stood at a distance. He would not even look up to heaven, but beat his breast and said, 'God, have mercy on me, a sinner.' I tell you that this man, rather than the other, went home justified before God"* (Luke 18:10-14).

Legalism confuses spiritual position and condition. It also goes on to spiritualize positions on everything from what music "styles" God accepts as real worship to what day of the week is the "legitimate" day to gather in worship. Legalism measures spirituality by how well we maintain and tenaciously hold to our interpretations and opinions concerning biblical truths which are not essential to salvation.

———— ⟡ ————

Legalism allows our differences in convictions about truths not essential to salvation to divide us and break fellowship.

It is not that we should abandon our convictions on certain things. For the Lord may very well be dealing with us uniquely in a way He does not need to with others. But we should never allow it to be the justification for strife and broken fellowship as members of the family of God who share a common parentage through new birth by the Holy Spirit.

Legalism encourages the notion that the more unwavering we are to our convictions and hold firmly to our spiritual opinions, the closer to God or more "spiritual" we are. And we can actually believe this—even if it means breaking fellowship with others who are members of the household of faith but who disagree with those positions. My wife coined the best definition of legalism I have ever heard. She called it, "The pride of being sanctified."

MODELS FOR SPIRITUAL MATURITY

In his book "Revolution Within; A Fresh Look at Supernatural Living," pastor and author Dwight Edwards identifies some popular approaches to spiritual maturity. Quoting from Larry Crabb's book "Connecting," he states them as follows:

"The first he calls the 'Do what is right' approach. This is the moralistic model and insists that people simply need to be exhorted to do what the Bible says. Changes come as people repent—turning away from the wrong and doggedly pursuing the right...At it's core it is an Old Covenant attempt at sanctification."

"The second approach he describes as 'Fix what is wrong.' This is the therapeutic model, which says people can't do what's right until damage from the past is looked at and healed. Change comes as people are repaired, namely by getting in touch with what's going on inside of them, facing their pain and disappointments, and courageously moving forward. Doing this requires help not provided by the Gospel."

"Third I would add yet another popular approach...which could be called 'Get what is missing.' This is the power encounter model. It continually seeks miraculous experiences with God as the key to spiritual growth." However he adds, "A faith that requires an ongoing diet of signs and wonders will never mature properly."

"A better model is... 'Release what is good.' Because of the New Covenant, there are supernatural resources permanently residing within the soul of every believer, and they're the source of all spiritual good. Whatever 'good' God wants to channel through us has already been placed within us; it simply awaits release....This is what Jesus was alluding to when He

80

promised, 'He who believes in Me, as Scripture has said, out of his heart will flow rivers of living water.' We're to allow the good (living water) to be released in a constant flow."

The source of all spiritual good is the ministry and power of the Holy Spirit who lives within. There are elements of truth to all of the models of spiritual maturity Dwight Edwards sights in his book. But the point is, a dynamic, growing relationship with Jesus is the key to sanctification and soul restoration. This relationship is made to be a personal reality by the presence and ministry of the Holy Spirit who is the "Spirit of Christ" (Romans 8:9).

As I drink of the *"still waters"* He leads me beside, I am sanctified because *"He restores my soul."* Soul restoration involves miracle healing and deliverance, recovery, truth, empowerment of will, change of mind and heart, embracing the will of God for my life, right relationships in the body of Christ, and more. But the point is, there is no such thing as a quick fix to soul restoration anymore than there is a point of arrival at full sanctification this side of heaven.

A DYNAMIC PROCESS

When the Lord shepherds my life, there is a growing conformity into the likeness of Jesus (Romans 8:29) and a growing up into Him in all things (Ephesians 4:15).

Again sanctification is a relationship outcome. I am sanctified by a life-long, miraculous, dynamic process of soul restoration in the context of a vital and growing relationship with the Good Shepherd. The apostle Peter emphasizes this truth. *"Though you have not seen Him, you love Him; and even though you do not see Him now, you believe in Him and are filled with an inexpressible and glorious joy, for you are receiving the goal of your faith, the salvation of your souls"* (1 Peter 1:8-9).

Peter is not speaking of "position" or standing before God for we receive this the moment we accept and confess Christ. But he is speaking of soul "condition" and a getting back to what was Adam's joy before the Fall. He is referring to something we are in the *process* of receiving. He states how our relationship with the Lord is a love relationship with One whom we've never seen.

RECOVERY AND DELIVERANCE

The result of this faith in and love for Christ is the process of soul restoration: *"receiving the goal of your faith, the salvation of your souls."*

A quick look at the original Greek meanings of three key words in this passage gives us the understanding of soul restoration as the outcome of the personal relationship we are cultivating with the Good Shepherd. *"Receiving"* (komizoo) means "to get back, to receive back what previously was one's own, to recover." *"Salvation"* (soteria) denotes "physical and moral safety, deliverance and health" *"Soul"* (psuche) means "the core of our being, the center of our thoughts, feelings, and decisions, the essence of our character."

The health and safety of our soul, as God originally intended and was Adam's condition before the Fall, is something we are recovering as part of our walk with Christ in the Spirit.

Soul restoration is directly proportionate to our intimacy with Christ, and it is evidenced by the kind of relationships we have with one another.

The health of Adam's soul was dependent upon God coming and walking and talking with him in the cool of the day. But in sin, Adam and Eve hid themselves and their souls lost the vital link of fellowship for health and wholeness.(Genesis 3:8-9). What was forfeited by the first Adam, we are now in the process of recovering through union with Jesus Christ, the second Adam (1 Corinthians 15:22,45).

SOUL RESTORATION BY THE POWER OF THE HOLY SPIRIT AND THE WORD OF GOD

The miracle of new birth is: we become a new creature, not a new and improved version of the old. *"Therefore, if anyone is in Christ, he is a new creation; the old has gone, the new has come!"* (2 Corinthians 5:17).

Again, quoting Dwight Edwards from His book "Revolution Within":

> *"Our flesh (is) that God-hostile, self-centered part of us often referred to as our 'fallen nature' or 'sin nature' or 'carnal nature.' Whether our flesh hangs out in church or at a bar, whether it's highly disciplined or self-indulgent, whether it's intoxicated by religious success or alcoholic drink, it is still flesh"* ... *'the flesh profits nothing' (John.6:63)...No amount of self-help, positive thinking, therapy, medication, or discipline will ever improve this nature...and will always have absolutely nothing to offer our spirituality."*

This reality of becoming a new creature, dominated by the Holy Spirit's influence rather than our fleshly nature, provided in the sinless life, atoning death and resurrection of Jesus, was a prophetic promise God announced through the prophet Ezekiel. *" I will give you a new heart and put a new spirit in you; I will remove from you your heart of stone and give you a heart of flesh. And I will put My Spirit in you and move you to follow My decrees and be careful to keep My laws"* (Ezekiel 36:26-27).

MORE THAN A MORAL CODE

God's gift at the new birth is a new mind, heart and will—not an improvement of the old one. And our human spirit comes alive to the ministry of the indwelling presence of the Holy Spirit. The instrument the Spirit of God uses to bring soul restoration is God's Word.

David knew this to be true when he wrote, *"The Law of the Lord is perfect, converting the soul"* (Psalm 19:7 NKJV).

When the Holy Spirit does His work of restoring, He empowers the new heart He has given us to return and embrace by faith the love and forgiveness of God in Christ as a lifestyle of repentance. This is why Christianity is a relationship and not just the intellectual comprehension and acceptance of a moral code of ethics and philosophical concepts about God, man and eternity espoused by Jesus.

The Bible doesn't say we believe in our mind. It says that by faith our heart embraces the truth. *"For it is with your heart that you believe and are justified, and it is with your mouth that you confess and are saved"* (Romans 10:10). The Holy Spirit also is the source of God's love to us. *"God has poured out His love into our hearts by the Holy Spirit whom He has given us"* (Romans 5:5).

The Holy Spirit also transforms our heart's affections and desires. Proverbs 21:10 says that *"the soul of the wicked desires evil."* 1 Peter 2:11 tells us it is our fleshly passions and desires which actually war against our soul to do it harm.

God's Spirit invests His holy passion for the glory of God and the good of others in our new heart to find it's satisfaction in new and healthy desires. *"My soul will be satisfied as with the richest of foods."* (Psalm 63:5). Psalm 103:5 NKJV declares that He is the God who *"satisfies your mouth with good things, so that your youth is renewed like the eagles."*

Since it is impossible for the carnal mind to understand and for the carnal will to obey, the Holy Spirit's work of soul restoration also includes the gift of a new mind that can receive and understand the revelational truths of God's Word and a will to obey.

The carnal mind of reason and the carnal will, dominated by selfish passions and desires, are enemies which fight against the soul-restoring ministry of the Holy Spirit. *"The sinful mind is hostile to God. It does not submit to God's law, nor can it do so. Those controlled by the sinful nature cannot please God. Since it is impossible for the carnal mind to understand and for the carnal will to obey, You, however, are controlled not by the sinful nature but by the Spirit, if the Spirit of God lives in you. And if anyone does not have the Spirit of Christ, he does not belong to Christ. But if Christ is in you, your body is dead because of sin, yet your spirit is alive because of righteousness. And if the Spirit of Him who raised Jesus from the dead is living in you, He who raised Christ from the dead will also give life to your mortal bodies through His Spirit, who lives in you"* (Romans 8:7-11).

"For the law of the Spirit of life in Christ Jesus has made me free from the law of sin and death" (Romans 8:2 NKJV). *"Do not conform any longer to the pattern of this world, but be transformed by the renewing of your mind. Then you will be able to test and approve what God's will is—His good, pleasing and perfect will"* (Romans 12:2). *"...But we have the mind of Christ"* (1Corinthians 2:16).

The Holy Spirit is at work in our soul empowering our will to relinquish control to Him and to accept the authority of God's Word—and for our values and thought process to agree with the truth of Scripture. To the degree we cooperate with this work and ministry of the Spirit, we experience the shepherding presence of the Lord in our lives restoring our soul.

THREE KEYS TO SPIRITUAL RELEASE AND SOUL RESTORATION

The disciplines of the Christian life are the way we cooperate with the soul-restoring work of the Holy Spirit. Bible reading, church attendance and prayer are activities included in that discipline. And yet our churches are filled with Christians who do these things and still struggle with *"throwing off everything that hinders and the sin that so easily entangles"* (Hebrews 12:1) as well as the unseen attitudes and heart issues the Bible calls *"contaminates of the spirit"* or the inner person (2 Corinthians 7:1).

There are some keys to releasing the Holy Spirit in our souls to accomplish this ministry. Although the following is not an all-inclusive list, there are three lifestyle disciplines which are vital to release the Holy Spirit's ministry in a soul-restoring way:

Key #1: A Lifestyle of Faith and Repentance.

Though our old selfish and prideful nature is subdued, is it not annihilated. Because of this fact, repentance is a lifestyle. And since this is true, we will never reach a state of complete sanctification until our old body of sin has been exchanged for a new glorified body like the Lord's which can stand eternally in His presence.

The three most difficult words for us to say are "I was wrong" or "I have sinned." Every time we are convicted by the Holy Spirit for a wrong to someone or a sin against the Lord, a little defense attorney in our mind stands up to defend our actions and attitudes; to justify, rationalize or compare ourselves to someone else who in our estimation has done things much worse than us.

But without repentance, there is no soul restoration. Other than His faithfulness to convict, the work of the Holy Spirit ceases at every point of disobedience. We never move beyond the current condition of our souls until we repent in accordance with the directive of God's Word in so far as our relationship to God and to others is concerned.

I had the uncomfortable task of finally approaching an associate pastor who was also a personal friend and call him into accountability for a certain action he had taken which had injured trust, raised questions of loyalty and sent a mixed message to the congregation and the church board.

When I asked him whether or not while in his senior pastoral role (at a previous church) any of his associates had conducted themselves in such a manner, he said "no." And when I asked why then he had conducted himself as such, his answer was, "Well, mistakes have been made." His ambiguous admission was neither repentant nor apologetic.

For all of us the most difficult thing is to personally own up to our wrong and our sin. The carnal nature's first impulse is always to duck through the door of rationalization.

Faith is nurtured by the Word of God. *"Faith comes from hearing the message, and the message is heard through the Word of God"* (Romans 10:17). However, the Word can only do it's sanctifying, soul-restoring work when it is humbly received and obeyed. *"Therefore, get rid of all moral filth and the evil that is so prevalent and humbly accept the word planted in you, which can save you"* (James 1:21).

Faith always obeys; it is an action not a disposition. Without humbly accepting the Word of God and responding in obedience to the voice of The Spirit in the Word, some sit in church or in front of the TV every week and hear the message but really never listen. They become "sermon junkies" looking for the next message preached to entertain them or worse yet, agree with their opinions. For them the Word of God does absolutely no good other than make them more responsible for having heard it.

Faith that disobeys becomes unbelief in two ways. It does what is contrary to the word of God and inconsistent with a walk with God. *"See to it, brothers, that none of you has a sinful, unbelieving heart that turns away from the living God"* (Hebrews 3:12). Or it leaves undone the good it has both the opportunity and the directive to do. *"Anyone, then, who knows the good he ought to do and doesn't do it, sins"* (James 4:17).

The lifestyle of faith and repentance releases the soul-restoring power of the Holy Spirit in our lives. He thrives in the heart that is humble, contrite, trusting and obedient.

Key #2: A Lifestyle of Love, Acceptance and Forgiveness.

We are not only sinners we are sinned against. The sinful actions, attitudes and words of others has a traumatizing effect upon our mind and heart.

We live in a fallen world of wrong and hurt and we are pained by it regularly to some degree or another. There is no deeper wound than love rejected. And for that reason alone, God is the chief sufferer of the universe. No one loves more perfectly and deeply than God. And yet there is no one whose love is scorned and rejected more than the Lord's.

Zechariah gives this prophetic and poignant image of the suffering Messiah: *"And one will say to Him, 'What are these wounds between Your arms?' Then He will answer, 'Those with which I was wounded in the house of My friends'"* (Zechariah 13:6 NKJV).

John's Gospel opens with, *"He came to His own, and His own did not receive Him"* (John 1:11 NKJV).

The agony and suffering of the Cross was our answer to Christ's life and ministry of love and blessing. My sin put Him there as surely as anyone else's at any point in human history. And it is from that perspective I must see my hurt and disappointment. I must bring my pain and rejection to the foot of the Cross and see what my sin cost Jesus.

My hurt, though very potent and real, pales in comparison with that of Christ. His Cross is not only God's most powerful display of love, acceptance and forgiveness for me, it is the reason why I offer love, acceptance and forgiveness to those who have sinned against me. In fact, offering it to others is the only evidence that I have really received it from the Lord for myself. Paul writes, *"And do not grieve the Holy Spirit of God, with whom you were sealed for the day of redemption. Get rid of all bitterness, rage and anger, brawling and slander, along with every form of malice. Be kind and compassionate to one another, forgiving each other, just as in Christ God forgave you"* (Ephesians 4:30-32).

Forgiveness is not a feeling, it is a decision.

I exist and act in agreement with this decision in order that forgiveness might be the antiseptic which keeps the wounds in my life clean until they heal. Such healing comes when I can remember the hurtful situation, but no longer feel the pain.

When I forgive in this way, the Holy Spirit's work of soul restoration is released in my own life in order to flow in blessing to others. 1 Samuel 24 is the account of David and his mighty men hiding from Saul in the very cave where Saul chose to sleep for the night. David had been appointed by God and anointed by Samuel to take Saul's place in leadership. This anointing had also brought power into David's life (1 Samuel 16).

Rather than kill Saul and put an end to his problems, David cut a corner off of Saul's robe as he slept to prove to Saul he had the power to take his life, yet didn't. It was not David's fear of Saul that stayed his sword. One look at the abilities of David's mighty warriors would give him no cause to fear. And it was not just his respect and reverence for the anointed office of king in Israel.

The real dynamic at work here was that David chose to walk in forgiveness toward Saul. We know this because David was grieved in his heart over his action. *"Now it happened afterward that David's heart troubled him because he had cut Saul's robe. And he said to his men, 'The LORD forbid that I should do this thing to my master, the LORD's anointed, to stretch out my hand against him, seeing he is the anointed of the LORD.' So David restrained his servants with these words, and did not allow them to rise against Saul"* (1 Samuel 24:5-7 NKJV).

David knew something of the soul-restoration he wrote about in His "shepherd's psalm."

I was called to pastor a church which had a ten-year history of division, strife and pain prior to my arrival. The church was behind in it's mortgage payment and I had invited a representative from the lending company to be present at the first annual business meeting to give the membership an appraisal of the situation. I discovered the depths of the difficulty only after assuming the pastorate.

About six months into my tenure, I began to realize something had to be done to bring healing or Christ's kingdom work could never be accomplished. I was informed that during the previous pastor's tenure, the church's denominational leadership had been called in to assist in quelling the difficulties and act in a conciliatory way to bring reason and order to warring factions. The result of that meeting was the pastor and board excommunicated a number of families from the church. All had received a letter restraining them from returning to the property. Some had been publicly excommunicated from the pulpit on Sunday.

I believed the Holy Spirit was directing me to arrange for a reconciliation service and invite all to attend who desired to give and receive love, acceptance and forgiveness. We provided a worship and fellowship gathering in the church sanctuary where a "declaration of reconciliation" was read and affirmed by all. During the worship and praise service that lasted at least thirty minutes, those who needed to go to others and give and receive forgiveness were encouraged to do so.

It was truly a divine encounter to witness those who hadn't spoken to one another in over a year go and tearfully embrace and make apologies in an environment of praise and worship. Communion was served and a fellowship meal was provided afterwards. The entire service lasted nearly four hours. Many just wanted to linger together in the sanctuary.

Only after this event did the church begin to experience growth and blessing. Today it is healthy and strong under new pastoral leadership.

You see, the Lord is more concerned about how we get along than He is concerned about what we do for Him. He is more interested in how we treat each other than how well we teach a Sunday School class or sing in the choir.

Jesus said if we know someone has a legitimate reason to be at odds with us, we are to take the initiative to go and be restored to such a person. Otherwise our gift of ministry will not be acceptable to Him.

Jesus' command (not a suggestion) was to leave our gift at the altar and go and be reconciled to our brother or sister (Matthew 5:23-24).

My ability to accept another is no longer according to my standards, but rather in accordance with what Christ has done for them. *"Therefore from now on, we regard no one according to the flesh…"* (2 Corinthians.5:16 NKJV).

Christ's acceptance of them is ours. *"To the praise of the glory of His grace, by which He made us accepted in the Beloved"* (Ephesians 1:6 NKJV). In this way social and racial barriers disappear in the love, acceptance, and forgiveness of Jesus Christ demonstrated through His people whose souls are being restored.

Key #3: A Lifestyle of Worship and Praise.

There is such a storehouse of well-written, expositive materials on the subject of worship and praise that any Christian who is a half-way serious worshiper can't help but realize worship and praise encompasses infinitely more than your favorite ten to twenty minute song service on Sunday.

Why is it then, when the Sunday morning music does not include our favorite choruses, hymns or appeal to our discriminating music taste, we give the worship service and worship leader a less than favorable rating?

Can we really blame someone else for how poorly we worship? Could it be that we aren't getting much out of it because our heart is putting very little into it? Have we considered how limited our expressions of worship and praise might really be, to place so much emphasis upon a twenty minute segment of time when we have had the entire week to express our love of the Lord in so many other ways?

The Old Testament word study and New Testament teaching on the subject tells us at the least our worship and praise includes the following expressions: vocal, instrumental, loud, soft, exuberant, reverent, fast, slow, private, public, with raised hands, clapping hands, making a joyful noise, shouting, dancing, bowing down, giving of our money, serving through our gifts, winning the lost, when we feel like it, when we don't feel like it, and the Christ-like example we set for others to follow.

Yet, with all of these Scriptural opportunities to give expression to worship and praise, we face a worship "style" crises in the church. Everywhere you see those of every denomination advertising on their marquee their offering of both "traditional" and "contemporary" worship services at different hours.

The nature of music itself, generational differences, and cultural distinctives probably have much to do with this. But the fact is that for many congregations the subject of worship "style" has literally become an emotion-laden disruption to what is to be the unified entering into the presence of the Lord in our worship gatherings.

———— ❦ ————

Worship and praise is part of the process of soul-restoration which God longs to bring to His people.

David's anointed worship brought the presence of God to dispel the oppression in Saul's life. It was a music style contemporary to his time I'm sure. But the presence of God was there solely because David was a worshiper, a man after God's own heart.

His life expressed worship and praise in a multitude of ways including both the song and the dance. It also manifest itself in sacrifice. David said, *"I will not sacrifice to the Lord burnt offerings that cost me nothing"* (2 Samuel 24:24).

In 2 Samuel 23, David shared a desire for a drink of water from the well of Bethlehem. Three of David's mighty men, over-hearing his request, broke through the military lines of the Philistines, risking their lives to secure the water for David's refreshment.

When he saw the warrior's display of devotion to him and how they were willing to risk their own lives just for a drink of water, he realized he was undeserving. It was nothing less than a gift from the Lord.

So rather than consume it himself, he poured the water out upon the ground in worship to God.

Whenever and wherever David saw the working of the Lord he worshiped. And it was in a spontaneity that was truly Spirit led. His worship life was not dependent upon a favorite music style in a weekly corporate praise gathering.

David wrote, *"As the deer pants for streams of water, so my soul pants for you, O God. My soul thirsts for God, for the living God. When can I go and meet with God?"* (Psalm 42:1-2). *"Then my soul will rejoice in the LORD and delight in His salvation. My whole being will exclaim, Who is like you, O LORD?"* (Psalm 35:9-10). What David was seeking was the presence of the Lord.

Paul described the soul restoration which comes to us as we enter His presence and look to Him in praise and worship. *"Now the Lord is the Spirit, and where the Spirit of the Lord is, there is freedom. And we, who with unveiled faces all reflect the Lord's glory, are being transformed into his likeness with ever-increasing glory, which comes from the Lord, who is the Spirit"* (2 Corinthians 3:17-18).

We emulate what we truly worship. It is amazing to see the image of Brittany Spears, Janet Jackson or any of the latest rock, pop or rap artists copied by young teens (girls and boys) through their adopted fashion styles. In fact, I watched a portion of a recent television special that featured young adults going under the knife with hopes the plastic surgeon's talents could shape and mold them into a respectable image of the specific motion picture star they idolized.

Grown-ups are part of the act too. When was the last time you watched a professional sporting event and the cameras didn't broadcast someone wearing body and face paint true to their team's colors. In fact, everywhere and every day the flash of team sportswear gives witness to the fervor of enthusiastic worshipers.

Others, by their lifestyle and appearance, emulate beauty, materialism, anti-socialism, pleasure, etc., as the idol of their heart's interest and affections.

Our worship and praise testifies to two things. It is a declaration to the world of what we think of our God and it testifies to the condition of our soul.

When the Lord shepherds our life, He inhabits our praise and worship, and the interchange brings restoration to our souls.

CHAPTER SEVEN

FINDING PURPOSE AND DIRECTION

"He leads me in paths of righteousness for His name's sake."
– PSALM 23:3 NKJV

T he path of life can sometimes seem like the description given by two road signs that alerted drivers to the highway ahead. A sign in central Oregon reads, "Soft Shoulder; Blind Curves; Steep Grade: Big Trucks; GOOD LUCK."

Another sign in the Mojave Desert reads, "Absolutely Nothing Next 22 Miles."

Although our road seems like this at times, according to the promise David presents, this is not what is ahead for the Christian believer. The path before us may have some treacherous curves, steep grades, and monster trucks but we have far more to depend on than "good luck." Even a "Mojave Desert" experience can be filled with the purpose and presence of the Lord.

The real world is the Bible world. *"For no matter how many promises God has made, they are 'Yes' in Christ. And so through Him the 'Amen' is spoken by us to the glory of God"* (2 Corinthians 1:20).

If we allow the things we feel humanly and think carnally to be the "highway sign" indicators of our road ahead, we will veer off God's path for our lives and park in a cul-de-sac of emotional and spiritual breakdown.

Unbelief will make the promises of God ineffective. We can even attend church and just sit and stare, unmoved by much of anything because of the resting spiritual inertia.

The promise, *"He leads me in paths of righteousness for His name's sake"* is one of the greatest reasons to hope and to be inspired about the future. It is the "highway sign" God has erected by the road He is leading everyone of His children on. And He has it illuminated by His Holy Spirit to let you know that in Him the best is always yet to come.

"ACTIVELY MOVING"

My life in Christ is not a rest stop to pull into, it is a pathway to journey on. A look at the meanings of the words in this text gives us this understanding. *"Leads"* (nachah/Hebrew) means to "lead forth or to bring forth." *"Paths"* (ma'gal/Hebrew) is interpreted as "a way, or a going." It indicates the Lord is always actively moving us forward in Him.

This is not an image which is contradictory to, *"He makes me to lie down in green pastures."*

————⟡————

Lying down in green pastures is not a picture of inactivity. It is the illustration of peace, rest and nourishment for the soul in order that we might remain active for God.

I am speaking of being active in praise, worship, prayer, fellowship with God's people, giving, serving, faith, ministering, helping others, building Christ's kingdom, encouraging, loving, spiritual growth, staying married and keeping your family together, following God-given leadership in the church and active in whatever God gives you the opportunity to do.

THE NATURE OF THE LORD'S GUIDANCE
God uses a number of sources to give us direction:

■ He speaks to us by His word preached, taught or read.

- He speaks to our hearts in prayer by the voice of His Spirit in more specific ways.
- He speaks to us through the supernatural utterance gifts of the Holy Spirit as we gather in corporate worship.
- He speaks to us through wise, Godly counsel from others who love us.
- He speaks through events and circumstances we experience.

Some or all of these can play a role in confirming God's direction. There are also a number of things to consider when walking through the decision-making process and the will of God. He gives us talents, interests and life motivations that suit us for specific usefulness to Him.

Ask yourself, "What would I like to do for God? What am I equipped to do for the Lord?" Once you've figured this out you still have to get off the couch!

He gives us life experiences which prepare us for service. Ask yourself, "What have I learned by the things I've been through that can be useful in helping others?" He generally stirs our hearts by the prompting of the Holy Spirit. He gives confirmations from Scripture as we seek to hear His voice in His Word, and then opens doors for us to consider.

The nature of the Lord's guidance includes the following four aspects:

1: God always leads us forward, not backward.

When David said, *"He leads me in paths,"* he was saying God always has a destiny for you and me and a way to get there. He is continually moving forward, not backward, to accomplish His will.

Any backward motion found in Scripture is a reference to us not to God, and it has to do with "backsliding." It means we stop moving forward in faith.

Great men of God experienced the angst in their own lives with regards to the Father's timetable. The question they all asked of God in their situation was *"How long?"* David questioned, *"How long, O*

LORD? Will You forget me forever? How long will You hide your face from me? How long must I wrestle with my thoughts and every day have sorrow in my heart? How long will my enemy triumph over me?" (Psalm 13:1-2). *" How long will the enemy mock You, O God? Will the foe revile Your name forever? Why do You hold back Your hand, Your right hand? Take it from the folds of Your garment and destroy them!"* (Psalm 74:10-11).

Jeremiah cried, *"How long must I see the battle standard and hear the sound of the trumpet?"* (Jeremiah 4:21).

Habakkuk inquired of the Lord, *"How long, O LORD, must I call for help, but You do not listen? Or cry out to You, 'Violence!' but You do not save? Why do You make me look at injustice? Why do You tolerate wrong? Destruction and violence are before me; there is strife, and conflict abounds. Therefore the law is paralyzed, and justice never prevails. The wicked hem in the righteous, so that justice is perverted"* (Habakkuk 1:2-4).

In heaven this is the cry of the martyred saints: *"I saw under the altar the souls of those who had been slain because of the word of God and the testimony they had maintained. They called out in a loud voice, "How long, Sovereign Lord, holy and true, until You judge the inhabitants of the earth and avenge our blood?"* (Revelation 6:9-10).

The point being, if you have ever questioned God concerning His ways or His timing you're on par with the greats of the Christian faith. I believe God welcomes any question as long as our fear and anxiety doesn't turn to unbelief which impugns His character. I know God certainly desires this dialogue.

The bottom line of every spiritual battle we face is our faith and trust in the Lord. What our spiritual adversary desires is the diminishment of our faith. Satan does this by calling into question the character of God when our circumstances seem to support that charge.

In all of this remember the Lord leads us down righteous paths. The devil drives us toward destructive detours.

2: There are no short cuts on this forward path in the Lord.

In fact, the shortest distance between two points in the will of God is always the path He leads me on. God may be beyond time and space but we are not.

The principle of stewardship taught in the Bible also has to do with the use of our time. In God's dealing with us He is never inconsistent with the principles of His Word—and the stewardship of time applies. The road God is leading us on only seems long and wearisome when it is not to our liking. Our time table is not God's. No matter how long He takes, God's path is still always the shortest.

For example, the direct route from Egypt to Canaan for the Israelites was not an unreasonably long trek. But the forty years of wilderness wandering, "boldly going nowhere" because of unbelief, self-will and rebellion against Moses most certainly was. Even Moses, as meek a man and as great an anointed leader as he was, couldn't drag the people kicking and screaming into God's promised destiny for them.

As it proved to be true for a generation of Jews in the wilderness, "Time may be a good teacher; unfortunately it kills all of its students."

Remember, the most direct route to anywhere is a street called "The Will of God."

3: *There are no emergency exits on the path where He leads.*

By this I mean the Lord never seems to answer the prayer, "Lord, get me out of this one!" He most generally "brings me through" each trial with a lesson learned, spiritual growth experienced and a new understanding of the ways of God's power and grace.

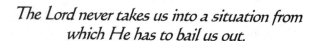

The Lord never takes us into a situation from which He has to bail us out.

Even when His grace and power miraculously brings us through times of distress, those state of affairs are most often ones we get ourselves into either by prayerlessness, ignorance, lack of discernment or pride and self will. They may also be situations the sinful actions of others have thrust upon us, or the oppression which can besiege our hearts and minds from encounters with our spiritual adversary—which is part and parcel of living in a fallen world. But they are not the places where the Lord specifically leads us to bring about defeat.

Not everything that happens to the Christian believer is good. Yet, by a faith-filled response and in prayer, we can invite God to work all these things for our good. This is His promise in Romans 8:28.

The Word of God declares *"When tempted, no one should say, 'God is tempting me.' For God cannot be tempted by evil, nor does He tempt anyone; "* (James 1:13-14). *"Now thanks be to God who always leads us in triumph in Christ, and through us diffuses the fragrance of His knowledge in every place"* (2 Corinthians 2:14 NKJV).

These passages together tell us God never tests or tempts us with evil. He never leads us into situations which have designs for our downfall. He always leads us into triumph in *all* things, no matter how they come our way. And those experiences and encounters with God serve as an opportunity to make the knowledge of Christ's love and power known to others, which Paul describes as a pleasant fragrance, which when diffused fills the atmosphere.

4: The Lord guides us personally.

David said, *"He leads me."*

There are many wonderful books which lay out the Biblical success principles of the Christian life. They can be called God's laws for victory, prosperity, harvest, healing, blessing and being a blessing, etc. But more than 'laws" of God, I believe these are "relationship outcomes" with the Father. Because the Christian life is more than learning a set of principles and then committing to apply a set of disciplines to our life.

The New Age mystic believes in peace and prosperity too, and principles for living which "tap into" the "source" of positive return in your life. They even make contact with "spirit guides" (demonic familiar spirits) for personal wisdom and instruction. But they know nothing of the promises of God that are ours only in right relationship with Christ Jesus (2 Corinthians 1:20).

God's personal presence is what He promised Moses and all of Israel. *"If You are pleased with me, teach me Your ways so I may know You and continue to find favor with You. Remember that this nation is Your people. The LORD replied, 'My Presence will go with you, and I will give you rest'"* (Exodus 33:13-14).

Jehovah didn't give Moses and the Israelites a map of the desert to decipher. He gave them His presence in the cloud of smoke by day and the pillar of fire by night. The Lord may not appear in fire and smoke today, but His promise of personal guidance for us is the same.

Guidance is made available by the Holy Spirit through intimacy and fellowship with Christ.

When Jesus was telling the disciples that His physical presence would be absent from them He assured them He would be present by His Holy Spirit. He told the disciples specifically that the Holy Spirit would guide them and be His voice. *"But when He, the Spirit of truth, comes, He will guide you into all truth. He will not speak on His own; He will speak only what He hears, and He will tell you what is yet to come. He will bring glory to Me by taking from what is Mine and making it known to you"* (John 16:13-14).

God promised to personally guide David and to give Him understanding. *" I will instruct you and teach you in the way you should go; I will guide you with My eye"* (Psalm 32:8 NKJV). *"Eye"* ('ayin/Hebrew) means "the literal eye, as well as mental and spiritual faculties."

The Lord was assuring David He would guide Him first by personally watching over him. He would also instruct David by giving him God's very own wisdom, understanding and spiritual insight as part of that process. This insight didn't just come from a book on successful living. David did have God's Word, but He also heard the voice of the Spirit. That is God's promise to all of us.

GOD'S DIRECTION FOR OUR LIVES: "PATHS OF RIGHTEOUSNESS"

David said, *"He leads me in paths of righteousness."*

The word *"righteousness"* (tsedeq/Hebrew) signifies "what is right; just in cause." It also includes the idea or the outcome of "deliverance, victory, prosperity."

God's direction will ultimately be just in cause as well as right for us personally. It will lead to the deliverance, victory and prosperity He has promised.

Our Heavenly Father knows us better than we know ourselves. And when He says the thoughts He thinks of us are for good not for evil, and the plans He has for us are not for harm but for a hopeful future (Jeremiah 29:11), this is His motive in all of His dealings in our lives. David reaffirms this truth when he states the Lord leads us in *"paths of righteousness."*

In retrospect, we could all look back and wish some things were different. The older you become the more you have a natural tendency to contemplate and wonder, "What if? or "If only!"

It is true that where we are today is the sum total of our choices. And all of our regrets in life can be identified as having been the decisions we made outside of the known will of God; choices which were inconsistent with a right relationship with Him, and the consequences they brought.

THOROUGHLY RESTORED

Even when the Lord is shepherding our lives, His *"paths of righteousness"* are sometimes the most trying, challenging and discomfiting ones because they require a walk of faith and obedience. But they are always paths which are right for us. And although there are some things we live with in the natural which are the result of wrong choices, God's forgiveness is complete and His grace is more than sufficient to heal and empower us for His will.

The temptation in times of failure is to try and make it up to God like we try and mend fences with those whom we have failed. But we can never make it up to God. In fact God has promised to recover what we have lost to bring Him glory and accomplish His will. He says, *"I will repay you for the years the locusts have eaten..."* (Joel 2:25).

The promise is that if we will turn to Him in repentance and faith, He will do a greater work in and through our lives of restoring, blessing and glorifying His name. It will more than compensate for any lost time and wasted opportunities. Such a marvelous work of grace serves to make us grateful worshipers even more.

The paths of righteousness the Lord leads me in will bring completeness and maturity to my life in preparation for eternity. When Paul speaks of perfection it has nothing to do with sinless or moral perfection. *"We proclaim Him, admonishing and teaching everyone with all wisdom, so that we may present everyone perfect in Christ"* (Colossians 1:28).

"Perfect" (teleios/Greek) is translated as "completeness, maturity." The writer to the Hebrews references Jesus as the *"Great Shepherd of the sheep"* whose leading us on a pathway of completeness to prepare us to do the will of God! *"Now may the God of peace who brought up our Lord Jesus from the dead, that great Shepherd of the sheep, through the blood of the everlasting coveant, make you complete (perfect) in every good work to do His will, working in you what is well pleasing in His sight, through Jesus Christ, to whom be glory forever and ever. Amen"* (Hebrews 13:20 NKJV).

Here, *"perfect/complete"* (kitartizoo/Greek) means, "completely prepared; thoroughly restored; to make one sound, fit, and what he ought to be."

"Every good work" does not just apply to this life, but to the eternal work the Lord has for us serving and reigning with Him in His kingdom.

———————— ✦ ————————

*The destiny God has for you and me is to share
His eternal throne of the universe.*

Jesus tells us, *"Do not fear, little flock, for it is your Father's good pleasure to give you the kingdom"* (Luke 12:32 NKJV). And Paul declares, *"If we endure, we shall also reign with Him"* (2 Timothy 2:12 NKJV). *"Do you not know that we shall judge angels?"* (1 Corinthians 6:3 NKJV).

John the revelator was given the vision of the servants of the Lord, the redeemed reigning in heaven with Christ. *"And there shall be no more curse: but the throne of God and of the Lamb shall be in it; and His servants shall serve Him: And they shall see His face; and His name shall be in their foreheads. And there shall be no night there; and they need no candle, neither light of the sun; for the Lord God giveth them light: and they shall reign for ever and ever"* (Revelation 22:3-5 NKJV).

This kind of destiny requires a lifetime of preparation. It is what *"paths of righteousness"* are truly about. As I make repentance my lifestyle, Christ's *"blood continually cleanses me from all unrighteousness"* (1 John 1:9 NKJV).

THE TEST OF FIRE

Paths of righteousness are not to keep me saved; it is faith in the blood of Jesus which does that. *"Paths of righteousness"* mature and prepare me for my eternal reward and the rank of rulership with Christ which awaits me.

Paul says there will be degrees of reward based upon how occupied we have been with kingdom life and kingdom work. *"...each one's work will become clear; for the Day will declare it, because it will be revealed by fire; and the fire will test each one's work, of what sort it is. If anyone's work which he has built on it endures, he will receive a reward. If anyone's work is burned, he will suffer loss; but he himself will be saved, yet so as through fire"* (1 Corinthians 3:13-15 NKJV).

The term *"work"* (ergon/Greek) indicates not only what one does, but what one is by occupation. It is one thing to play baseball, it is quite another to be a baseball player.

When *"He leads me in paths of righteousness,"* I stop merely attending a church service, and I began to be of service to Christ. That is the point! I will enter the next world of heaven's Kingdom as much a candidate for reward (and as prepared to rule with Christ) as I am when I leave this world. His shepherding influence and the *"paths of righteousness"* I follow Him in make the difference.

GOD'S PURPOSE FOR OUR LIVES: "FOR HIS NAME'S SAKE"

What's in a name? Browsing through a name book is a reminder that what we are called has consequences.

Once you discover the meaning and derivation of the arrangement of vowels and consonants which make up your name, you sense to some degree an identity, whether you live up to it or not. Names can be revered or they can be notoriously scandalized by the life and character of the previous person who bore that name. For example, how many girls have you met with the name Delilah? How many boys have you been introduced to named Judas?

The Bible declares God's name is "holy." It is the holiness of God which makes Him so unlike us. The term *"holiness"* (qodesh/Hebrew) means "separateness or set-apartness." His holiness—or "otherliness" sets Him apart from us and all of His creation. It is the blazing white hot purity of God which is infinitely separate from sin and evil. *"Your eyes are too pure to look on evil. You cannot tolerate wrong..."* (Habakkuk 1:13).

God's holiness can make us uncomfortable with Him. It is why the Pharisees had such a problem with Jesus. They laid claims to be the holy churchmen of Israel until the "Holy One" of Israel showed up and blew their cover. He did more than threaten their religious system, whose practices and codes were absurd extrapolations of the Law given to Moses at Mt. Sinai (Matthew 23:1-24). He said that hookers and crooked IRS agents would get into heaven before these religious people would (Matthew 21:31). He exposed what a sham their claim to holiness was.

The Bible declares God's name is *"Holy"*—and it is in the context of His inherent mercy, grace, and redemptive love toward us. When we speak of *"for His name's sake"* in Psalm 23, we are talking about the honor and glory of His name as He has associated with us. *"For... sake"* (ma'am/Hebrew) denotes "on account of, to the intent that." *"Name"* (shem) is defined as "a mark or memorial of individuality, honor, character, authority, reputation."

In 2 Chronicles 7:14 the Lord expresses His desire to associate His name with His people in terms of having called them by His name. David states, *"He provided redemption for His people; He ordained His covenant forever—holy and awesome is His name"* (Psalm 111:9).

HIS HOLY NAME

Mary's song of praise declares His name *"holy"* as she celebrates God's provision of mercy to future generations through the Incarnation. *"For the Mighty One has done great things for me—holy is His name. His mercy extends to those who fear Him, from generation to generation"* (Luke 1:49-50).

It is the lesson Jesus was teaching the disciples when James and John wanted to call down fire from heaven to consume those villages which had not received the Lord's ministry. Little wonder Jesus named them *"sons of thunder"* (Mark 3:17).

Mark tells us how Jesus responded. *"But He turned and rebuked them, and said, 'You do not know what manner of spirit you are of. For the Son of Man did not come to destroy men's lives but to save them'"* (Luke 9:55-56 NKJV).

The point was that the glory of God's holy name is demonstrated in the salvation of humanity not in its destruction. It's the same lesson God gave Moses when He requested to be shown the glory of God. The response of the Almighty was to cover and protect him as He passed by. But in doing so, God revealed His glory in the declaration of His grace and mercy. *"And He said, 'I will make all My goodness pass before thee, and I will proclaim the name of the LORD before thee; and will be gracious to whom I will be gracious, and will show mercy on whom I will show mercy* (Exodus 33:19 KJV).

It is because of His holiness there is absolutely no approach to Him except in the way He has prescribed.

This specific path has been provided through personal faith in the shed blood of Jesus Christ as atonement for our sin. *"Therefore, brothers, since we have confidence to enter the Most Holy Place by the blood of Jesus, by a new and living way opened for us through the curtain, that is, His body, and since we have a great priest over the house of God, let us draw near to God with a sincere heart in full assurance of faith, having our hearts sprinkled to cleanse us from a guilty conscience and having our bodies washed with pure water"* (Hebrew 10:19-23).

In Christ we have acceptance with a holy God. *"To the praise of the glory of His grace, by which He made us accepted in the Beloved"* (Ephesians 1:6 NKJV).

"FOR EVERY GOOD WORK"

When David writes, *"He leads me in paths of righteousness for His name's sake,"* the Holy Spirit is saying, God—on account of, for the honor of His character and reputation (i.e., *"for His name's sake"*)— redeems us by the shed blood of His Son Jesus, imparts His holiness to us by the indwelling presence of His Holy Spirit, and then leads us down paths which equip us to rule and reign with Him eternally.

In other words, God has staked His eternal reputation and the honor of His holy name on His work of redeeming a lost humanity and sharing His eternal throne with them. "Paths of righteousness for His name's sake" are those experiences when God in His love, grace, power and sovereignty, moves us forward in our Christian life to mature and better equip us for every good work here on earth as He prepares us to rule and reign with Him in His coming Kingdom.

This is also a process which changes the environment around us and has an impact upon others for the glory of God. We need to understand that no matter what circumstances the Lord orchestrates or allows in this forward walk, if He is truly shepherding our lives they are always *"paths of righteousness."*

In such paths the Holy Spirit *"always leads us in triumphal procession in Christ and through us spreads everywhere the fragrance of the knowledge of Him"* (2 Corinthians 2:14-15).

"OUR TRAGEDY—OUR TRIUMPH"

Jeff and Cris and their three children were members of a church I pastored for a number of years. The path the Lord led them in is a story that in Cris's own words is titled, "Our Tragedy—Our Triumph." It truly was as a *"path of righteousness"* as I have defined it. But at times that's the last thing it seemed to be. It is one of those circumstances when, as a pastor, you are called to walk down a *"path of righteousness for His name's sake"* with those whom God has given you to love and care for that mocks a common sense explanation while your moving forward.

Cris relates the story in her own words:

Jeff and I were living our dream. We had relocated from Southern California to the Pacific Northwest five years prior to begin a new life. We thought we had it all. We did have it all! As a wife and mother I had much to be thankful for. The love of a fine man, three beautiful children and a large, beautiful new home we just built. I was even fortunate enough to be a stay-at-home mom—something we were proud of and I didn't take for granted. On top of this we had begun a new relationship with the Lord two years earlier. We were truly blessed. However, what began as a day of promise turned out to be the darkest day of our lives.

It was Jessica's first day of first grade. So Jessica and the boys, (Eric and Evan), and I began our day with great anticipation. Evan (three years old) was the last to arrive at the breakfast table still wiping the sleep from his eyes. He reached up for his morning hug and as I knelt to the floor holding him in my arms, I remember how I wished that moment could last. But we were running late and I had to get a move on. Little did I know that would be the last time I would hold Evan in my arms alive.

When we arrived at school Evan was eager to explore and discover everything in Jessica's classroom as if it were his first day. In fact, he cried when it was time to finally go. Eric, Evan and I returned home and went about our daily routine. I was getting caught up on laundry and the boys were outside riding bikes up and down our driveway like so many times before.

I went outside to check on the boys and get the mail. On my way back I noticed Evan had a mischievous look on his face while riding his bike in circles in the garage. So I asked him "Whatcha' doing?"

"I just playing," he replied. "Okay! You be good now," I said, as I rustled my hand through his hair.

Not three or four minutes later Eric walked in. I thought it odd he was alone as Evan was always right behind him. So I asked, "Where's Evan?"

"In the garage," Eric replied. "What's he doing?" I questioned. "Playing," he said.

"Playing what?" I asked as I began to worry.

"He's hanging on the car," Eric replied.

I had locked the van when we got home as Evan's latest adventure was getting into the cars to play. Since it was getting warm and we were going back out later to pick Jessica up from school, I rolled the windows partially down to keep the van from getting too hot.

I dropped what I was holding and ran out to the garage. To my shock and horror there was my precious boy suspended only by his neck, his head wedged in the partly opened window of our van. He was unconscious and turning blue. Evan had used his tricycle, standing on it trying to get into the van through the partly opened window. As he poked his head through the window, the trike must have slipped out from under him, lodging his head between the window and doorframe.

I kept screaming, "Oh my God!" over and over. I had to get him out of there! I was in the state of shock and disbelief as I carried his lifeless body into the house. It was as if I were watching it happen to someone else. Like an out-of-body experience. Only it was real and it was happening to me.

I grabbed the phone and dialed 911 as I watched my child lay dying (if not already dead) on the floor, his breathing stopped. I began to get hysterical trying to explain what happened to him over the phone knowing it was just a waste of precious moments. I screamed, "Just tell me how to do CPR on a three year old boy!"

The dispatcher walked me through the steps as she verified the address I was calling from. I did just what she said but my efforts were in vain.

The next thing I knew the Fire Chaplain arrived. Before I could even respond, three paramedics were upon us. They immediately began CPR and when I saw them tear Evan's clothing off to get the bag valve respirator started, I fell to my knees sobbing in prayer, barely able to breath myself. Eric (four years old) became frightened and began crying as well.

Just at that moment the phone rang and the Chaplain answered. It was a friend, Debbie Williams, the wedding coordinator from church calling to see if I would be interested in helping out at an upcoming wedding. The Chaplain explained to her what was happening and asked if she could get someone over here to take me to the hospital. That one phone call started a chain of events.

The Chaplain then telephoned my husband Jeff who had to be called out of a meeting. He only told him there had been an accident with the van and Evan was hurt. He then prayed with me. Everything happened so fast.

As the paramedics wheeled Evan out of the house they gently explained they had managed to get a heartbeat but it was very faint. Evan was in a coma with serious brain damage. I was numb.

Once at the hospital I was escorted to what felt like an interrogation room. Surrounded by two doctors, a nurse and a social worker, the doctors started asking questions. "How long do you think he was alone?" "How long was he unconscious?" "What time frame was it from the last time you *saw him until you found him again?"*

I was scared to death and started to tremble. I felt like they were blaming me, and all I could think of was, "They're going to take my children away from me. I'm going to lose my family because they think I'm a bad mother." I told myself, "Choose your words wisely, Cris."

My answers were short. I gave them the information they needed and asked if I could see my baby.

Just as I walked out of the room Jeff arrived. I'll never forget the look of panic and fear on my husbands face. To have to tell my husband what happened was even more heartbreaking. I started crying again as I explained to him. His response was a gift from God. He put his hands on my shoulders, looked me in the eye and lovingly with compassion said, "This is NOT your fault. Do you understand? It's not your fault!"

I realized others from our church were there. Pastor Terry and Lin, Tim and Teresa who worked at the church school where Jessie attended, and the youth pastor and his wife. We finally got to see Evan and were told that his brain damage was extensive and that he would be 'life-flighted' to a Hospital in Seattle. They were better equipped to handle the trauma Evan suffered. They didn't offer much hope of recovery. We prayed over Evan.

Once at Children's Hospital we were escorted to Evan's room in the Intensive Care Unit. The nurses and physicians were so caring and compassionate. One of the nurses said: "He looks like a busy little guy. I'll bet he keeps you on your toes, doesn't he mom? He likes to play outside a lot doesn't he? I can tell by his tanned skin?"

I could only nod and smile as I thought of the times I'd have to run after him. I wished he would just wake up so I could see him play again. We were told that the first twenty-four hours were the most critical and that we may want to gather family members now since they were all out of state. Evan may not make it through the night. So the family was called and they came, some scheduling flights from quite a distance to be there. With everyone there we prayed and hoped for a miracle.

Our Senior Pastor Terry and Lin (his wife) were incredible. I remember thinking "How is this man going to counsel us when he has no children of his own?" However, the words he spoke were truly from God. They not only comforted us but also sustained us in the days and weeks that passed. One of the things that stayed with us was "God knows what you're going through. He knows your pain. He has also lost a son."

This was so profound to me as I was a young Christian. Just the look on Pastor's face and the emotion I knew he felt was evidence from God that he was not only trying to be there for Jeff and me, but was truly affected by this tragedy.

*J*eff and I were at Evan's side until very late that first night. They gave us a room to rest in that was located one floor above Evan's room. We lay in bed and slept for a couple of hours until I was awakened by the sound of Evan's voice. I dreamed he was standing in an open space with a glowing light all around him. He was smiling that radiant smile of his and yelled "Mommy, come watch me!" and then turned and ran off like he used to do. His voice was as clear as if he were right next to me.

I sat up and told Jeff I had to go see him and make sure he was still alive. When we got downstairs Evan's countenance had changed. He looked as though he were almost smiling. I believe the Lord was trying to tell me that Evan wasn't coming back to us. I never left his side again.

One of the nurses helped me get him out of bed so I could hold and rock him in the glider chair. We were told that with serious brain damage the body goes either very cold or very hot because the brain cannot regulate the body temperature. Evan's temperature at one point was 110 degrees. We tried gently patting him down with cool, wet cloths to help bring the temperature down but it was in vain. We had to apply

Vaseline to his eyes and mouth as well to keep them from drying out.

I remember singing to him a lot the second day and reading stories to him about Jesus. He used to sing, "Jesus loves me this I know, E-I-E-I-O," like the ending to the "Old McDonald's" song. So I sang "Jesus Loves Me."

Evan's health deteriorated as the hours passed by. While alone with him I tried to make a deal with God. "Please God, I don't care how you give him back to me. Just bring him back." But as I gazed at my son's face I knew I could not bear to have him back any other way but whole. Later, I would find that my husband Jeff had prayed a similar prayer. "Either bring him back all the way or take him home."

We knew it was up to the Lord. Later that day we were visited by a man who talked to us about organ donation. He wanted Evan's heart and kidneys and whatever useful organs they could harvest. I wanted to scream at him to go away and leave my child alone! He left us alone for a few moments so Jeff and I could talk it over. But our minds were already made up. We had no peace in taking Evan off of life-support. We wanted to give God every opportunity for a miracle so the answer was 'No'. After the man left Evan's room, I immediately went and vomited.

When night came and we were overcome with the need to sleep, Jeff went upstairs to rest for a few hours. As I held Evan in my arms I begged and pleaded with him to wake up and come back to me. I told him I was sorry that I wasn't there for him. As I lay in the bed next to him, Evan's breathing became more and more labored as the night progressed. Even with the life-support his little body was giving out. I could feel him slowly slipping away from me. At around 4:15 A.M. the nurse came in and said it was time to get Jeff and any other family members.

I ran to get Jeff and we decided we didn't want anyone else to be there. We helped the nurse remove all the wires and ventilation tube. Then Jeff held me as I held our baby and we watched him slowly take his final breaths in this life.

The attending nurse was so moved that she wanted to do something. She said, "I have an idea," and quickly left the room only to come back with a tin that said "My baby's hand to cherish." It was one of those kits that you mix with water to get a lasting handprint.

To this day I have Evan's little handprint as a reminder of how big he was when he died.

Pastor Terry and Lin drove us back to our house and there was a whirlwind of activity. Several of our neighbors, friends and our family were there to greet us. Once again, I was overwhelmed by all the love and support from those around us.

For me, planning Evan's funeral was almost worse than letting him go at the hospital. It meant this was really final. He was never coming back. I would never hold him in my arms again. Never see his smile or hear his voice. Our dreams were completely shattered and our lives forever changed.

We said our final goodbyes to Evan less than a week after the accident. Attending your own child's funeral—well there are absolutely no words to describe it. However, we were sustained by God's love through the wonderful people of our congregation as well as strangers in our community. I've never before or since then seen such an outpouring of love and support. We were weak with emotion and their love is what carried us through the events of that day. The sanctuary for the memorial service was so full that it was standing room only.

I was 37 years old and Jeff was 40 when we were talking about maybe having a third child. Then we found out I was pregnant. God decided we needed a third. Deciding on his name was easy since Evan means "precious gift from God." He was quickly dubbed "Evan, our baby from heaven." Now he would be "Evan, our angel in heaven."

Losing a child shatters you as a person, as a parent, as a spouse. It even threatens to shatter your faith in God. It will *either destroy you or make you stronger. To suffer the loss of a child is the cruelest most devastating thing a parent can go through. It's unexpected. It's not right. It's not the natural order of things. It's almost impossible to accept.*

Thankfully for us, we drew closer together and closer to God. We also decided to try to keep things as normal as possible for Jessie and Eric's sake. But what was "normal" anymore?

The little "three year old spark" in our family was gone. We were missing the one that always "stirred the pot." The one that kept us on our toes. We had to find a new "normal."

The first three or four months after Evan's death I was completely numb. I was just going through the motions of daily life. The only thing that got me out of bed in the morning was the fact that I had two other children who needed me. Thankfully, there was still a great deal of support from our church family and neighbors. I never had to cook a meal, other than breakfast for the kids, for at least eight weeks. And there were wonderful souls who often stopped by or sent cards and letters for a long time.

When the numbness started fading after the first few months I began to drink alcohol heavily. You see, I believe that God gives us a kind of an "insulation" when tragedy hits. We cannot absorb it all at once. It's too painful. It would kill us if we did. But I wanted to stay numb. I didn't want to deal with it. So I began drinking at least a bottle of wine every night. I would have my first glass around 4:30 P.M. when I started making dinner, and I wouldn't stop until it was time to go to bed. At night to help me sleep, I would take Tylenol PM on top of the wine.

No one in my house knew it. Not even my husband Jeff. The emotional and physical toll of losing Evan was immense. Even with all the alcohol and drugs in my system I would still wake up with tense muscles from my shoulders up to my ears. The first eighteen months after Evan died were a real strain on our marriage as well.

It's been ten years since Evan's death and there is still a hole in my heart. Every birthday, every new school year, every holiday is met with both joy and sorrow. Yet in spite of our tragedy, I believe with all my heart that God sent Evan Andrew to enrich our lives and to give us and those who knew him a small glimpse of eternity.

THE TURNING POINT

During those first eighteen months and afterward, Cris and Jeff struggled to find purpose and direction in this human tragedy which seemed like anything other than *"paths of righteousness for His name's sake."*

The Holy Spirit spoke into Jeff's life bringing the comfort that God understood his pain intimately for He too had lost a Son. Jeff received the faith and confidence to turn to the Lord in His sorrow and grief. He also was impressed with the truth that God had also received His Son again.

Jeff's son, Evan would never be lost to drugs, alcohol, or worse, lost to the kingdom of God because of sin and rebellion. Evan was in heaven, preserved for him. And just as God the Father, he too would receive his son back to himself again. Evan wasn't lost, he was just away for a while.

As I remember, a turning point came for Cris when in her deepest despair and all alone in a darkened bedroom she cried out to the Lord in prayer and asked for His help. Cris says, her room suddenly was bathed in an unexplainable manifestation of light, and the warmth of the presence of the Lord could be felt bringing to her soul a healing and delivering comfort. That was the end of her dependence upon alcohol to help her cope and drugs to help her sleep.

The purpose and direction began to come as Cris decided to celebrate her son's life while mourning his death. She had become emphatic about leaving Evan's bedroom untouched, including a closet full of clothes. She decided to take his clothes, cut them in pieces and artfully create a memorial quilt. She had enough to make decorative memory pillows for each of her other two children as well.

They made a special trip to see my wife and I to show us the quilt and share with us what the Lord was doing in their lives through this experience.

Cris, by her own admission, never considered herself cut out to be a great mom or child care provider. For a time she had a career, but when Evan was born, she directed her energies toward home. The last thing that Cris ever wanted to do was help in the church nursery. Coming to church was almost her oasis for a few hours of refreshing worship and fellowship. Not out of guilt but out of a sense of calling, she became the church's nursery coordinator and took this ministry to a new level.

One other important purpose this tragedy served was the healing of years of strained relationship between Cris and her mother. Cris said, "God sent Andrew Evan to enrich our lives...and to give us a small glimpse of eternity!"

The outcome of a fresh and vivid look at this life in light of eternity, the dynamic discovery of the Holy Spirit's healing and comforting presence, and significant spiritual and relational growth characterized their *"path of righteousness for His name's sake."*

---

*In the midst of a young mom and dad's
most confusing and painful experience imaginable,
purpose and direction was found.*

For all who allow His shepherding presence to be their life's greatest influence, even the most insanely unfair and personally devastating tragedies can be a living testimony to the truth that in all things, *"He leads me in paths of righteousness for His name's sake."*

CHAPTER EIGHT

FINDING THE POWER TO CONFRONT THE FORCES OF HELL

"Even though I walk through the valley of the shadow of death, I will fear no evil, for You are with me; Your rod and staff they comfort me."
– PSALM 23:4

Whenthe Lord shepherds my life I am equipped and empowered to fearlessly confront the impact sin has made upon this world, and the influence the intelligent, unseen forces of Hell continue to exert upon the culture around me and in the lives of people I encounter.

I maintain *"the valley of the shadow of death"* is more than the experience of our passing from this life into the next. It includes every day of our lives lived on this earth. The Fall, with the entrance of sin, the resultant depravity of the human soul and death to the human spirit and the aging of the body that will inevitably terminate in death for all of us, has made this entire planet the *"valley of the shadow of death."*

Like you, I sit in front of the television and feel the mind-numbing effect from the onslaught of reports which bring the traumatic sights and sounds that echo in this valley. Included are images such as Islamic terrorists beheading their victims in front of a camera that broadcasts to the world sadistic praise to a false god who holds the hearts and wills of millions of its devotees in a tireless grip.

- Or the report of at least seventy five serial killers who have been profiled in the United States by law enforcement agencies, and at this moment remain unidentified and un-detained, at liberty to take life randomly.
- Or the calculated and brutish butchering of trusting wives by monstrous husbands, irrespective of the fact that in one case a wife was carrying in her womb the best and most sacred thing which had come from their relationship; an unborn child.
- Or the fact there are 400,000 registered sex offenders in America with an estimated 100,000 more not registered.

These are the extreme manifestations to be sure. However, they play out against the backdrop of statistical indicators that profile our culture in general including the divorce rate, drug, alcohol and sexual addictions, teen pregnancy, abortion, the scandals in church, government and corporate business and the hedonistic excesses of the rich in stark contrast to the suffering of those in abject poverty. One almost becomes weary and depressed just picking up the morning newspaper.

SIN HAS MADE THIS WORLD THE VALLEY OF THE SHADOW OF DEATH

The psalmist didn't say "when I walk." He said *"though I walk through the valley of the shadow of death."* David, an adulterer and conspirator to murder, knew by experience what kind of a *"valley of the shadow of death"* sin in his own life and sin in the lives of others around him had made, even of his kingdom in Israel.

While in the most peaceful and prosperous of times, he knew of the constant threat of invading armies, inspired by Hell to conquer the Hebrew race and occupy the land promised to them by God in order to prove to the rest of the world the God of Israel was a liar.

Under the anointed inspiration of the Holy Spirit, David described this post-Eden world precisely with the phrase *"the valley of the shadow of death."*

THE SCOURGE OF SIN

The New Testament substantiates the claim that sin has made this world like unto the dark valley of which David speaks. Let me give you a few examples:

Paul states, *"...as sin entered the world through one man (Adam), and death through sin..."* (Romans 5:12). John writes, *"We know...that the whole world is under the control of the evil one"* (1 John 5:19). Jesus calls Satan *"the prince of this world"* (John 14:30). And Paul tells us that sin has made an impact upon the human soul so deep that he calls it *"the mystery of iniquity"* (2 Thessalonians 2:7).

Jesus says the place where He would build His church would be at *"the gates of Hell"* (Matthew16:18). He also lets us know that the closer we come to the hour of His return, the international, ecological, societal and human shock will be felt in even greater intensity from *"wars and rumors of wars, famines, pestilences, earthquakes, persecution of the church, real love growing cold, and lawlessness increasing"* (Matthew.24:6-14).

Paul prophesies that society's character under the growing impingement of sin's influence will be as *"terrible and savage times."* He declares, *"People will be lovers of themselves, lovers of money, boastful, proud, abusive, disobedient to their parents, ungrateful, unholy, without love, unforgiving, slanderous, without self-control, brutal, not lovers of the good, treacherous, rash, conceited, lovers of pleasure rather than lovers of God— having a form of godliness but denying its power"* (2 Timothy 3:1-4).

The apostle says sin has had such an oppressive affect upon the cosmos itself that creation was subjected to depravity and it eagerly awaits the change of the oppressive environment that will come when the Lord returns to rule with the saints and the sons of God are finally manifested (Romans 8:19-20).

STILL WALKING IN THE VALLEY

The Hebrew word for *"valley of the shadow of death"* is "tsalmaveth," meaning, "shadow of the grave or shade of calamity."

121

This can read as a poetic description of the Christian's passing from this life into the next. But it also is a picture of the world which sin has left us to live in every day of our lives. Iniquity has placed us in "the shade of calamity" and has made this place called earth the *"valley of the shadow of death"* which we have no choice but to walk through.

We can reside in a gated community with the best security alarm system installed, but we still have to travel the streets of our city. And we are still required to pay taxes to cover the staggering financial strain the cost of prisons and governmental social, health and welfare services exert upon the economy to address our society's pathologies.

The World Health Organization reports that worldwide, one in every two hundred adults is infected with HIV (not to mention the total accumulative amount of all other STD's). And the Center for Disease Control is continuously warning and monitoring the outbreaks of new disease epidemics such as SARS, Ebola, flesh-eating bacteria and the Asian bird flu. Sickness is so widespread that the availability of affordable healthcare to the citizens of nations is costing governments threatening proportions of their wealth and productivity to subsidize.

Yes, we are walking through "the valley of the shadow of death."

The Bureau of Justice Statistics reports that nearly 3% of the U. S. population has been incarcerated in state or federal prisons, with over 230,000 offenders convicted of rape or sexual assault, the medium age of the victim being 13 years of age. And according to a 2002 survey by the National Criminal Justice Reference Service, 23% of 8th graders, 41% of 10th graders and 59% of 12th graders reported how readily available to them were "club drugs" like Ecstasy and a variety of other methamphetamines (in addition to supplies of cocaine, marijuana and alcohol). In 1995, at a crime peak, it reported violent crimes in the U.S. to be at 1.8 million; 23% being between members of the same family. And the same bureau reports that of the children under 5 years of age murdered from 1976-2000, 31% were killed by their fathers, 30% killed by their mothers and 7% killed by other relatives. Again, we are walking through *"the valley of the shadow of death."*

When mass graves of tens of thousands of political murders are unearthed in Africa and Iraq—precious lives taken for the expedience of government control and the convenience of empowerment through fear—and when western civilization must live under the 24-hour threat of weapons of mass destruction and bio-terrorism, we are walking certainly through *"the valley of the shadow of death."*

IS THERE A SOLUTION?

A non-offensive, soft-sell of the Gospel, appealing to a segment of American society for whom the materialistic "American Dream" has become a reality, is legitimate and absolutely essential because successful and affluent people need Jesus too. But for the majority of Americans and citizens of third world countries, life in *"the valley of the shadow of death"* is much more a bleak reality they wake up to every morning and walk through every day.

The answer is not another government program, lax drug laws, another alcoholic beverage, a snort from a flavored oxygen bar, yoga exercises to medicate our pain or to relax our fragile psyches, new age mysticism to help us transcend the harshness of a real world or another promiscuous sexual relationship. It is the love, grace and power of the risen Jesus Christ.

The solution is found in the indwelling presence of His Spirit to bring real life change and to release us from the bondage of sinful strongholds. It is the truth of the word of God to bring life direction and stability and hope for the future. It is the friendship and unconditional love of Christian believers. It is the very presence of the Good Shepherd who promises, *"I am with you always, even unto the end of the age"* (Matthew.28:20 NKJV). It is He who will lead us fearlessly on this walk through *"the valley of the shadow of death."*

It was into this valley, *"in the fullness of time"* (Galatians 4:4-5) the eternal heir to the throne of David, the Good Shepherd, Jesus Christ the Messiah, Son of God and son of man, came as the first one to confront the dominions of Hell in order to *"destroy the works of the devil"* (1 John 3:8).

He came to release a redeeming, delivering and healing presence and power that alone could—and would—reverse the trends of depravity, delusion, despondency and overcome death itself.

CHRIST'S KINGDOM AUTHORITY IN THE VALLEY OF THE SHADOW OF DEATH

Let me share a supernatural experience I had as a pastor. It illustrates the reality of the truth that Jesus has released the power of His Spirit in this world to victoriously confront the forces of Hell. The story includes a number of specific situations which demonstrate the power of Christ's kingdom operating in this "valley."

I share this to encourage those who all too often feel despair and sense defeat, to take the spiritual offensive. I also share this to bring into focus the power and presence of Christ who is at work in this world so that evil, which often manifests a suffocating oppressiveness, should be no cause for us to fear.

One Sunday morning a well-dressed woman of eastern Indian decent responded to an altar call I had given. She came forward and received Jesus Christ as her personal Savior. I met her for the first time as she was accompanied by a man from our church who had invited her to the worship service. He was an insurance salesman who, while in the course of conversation, also became aware of the turmoil in her life and marriage.

She continued to attend our church, and on a regular basis would come forward after the service and ask for specific prayer for her husband.

One Sunday morning at the conclusion of the meeting, she came once again to the altar. Only this time she followed closely behind a small-framed gentleman also of eastern Indian descent. They approached the front of the sanctuary down the center aisle. The husband we had been praying for was now standing before me.

I greeted him and asked what I could do for him. He requested prayer because the doctors had told him he was not well. Although he smelled of alcohol, I proceeded to ask what the doctor's diagnosis was. When he refused to specify his need, I said, "Your problem is alcohol and what your are drinking is killing you." I explained I was not trying to embarrass him, but that I wanted to know how honest he would be concerning his need.

I quietly stated, "I am willing to pray for you, only if your are willing to give up the alcohol and trust Christ for salvation and deliverance."

That morning he received Christ and immediately knew something had changed inside him. Later he told us he had previously witnessed such a dramatic change in his wife, he came to church to find out what it was all about.

The gentleman went through detoxification at a hospital, and once released he never touched a drop of alcohol again. One Sunday morning, he testified with his wife standing by his side how his god had been alcohol for over thirty years. And now Jesus Christ was the Lord of his life.

He began the process of going back to work, recovering his driving privileges and being restored to healthy and productive living. For weeks I observed him in Sunday services, standing with hands raised, countenance bright, being one of the last to be seated after the time of musical worship and praise. He had truly been transformed by the miracle power of the Gospel of Jesus Christ.

Then one Sunday he came forward with the insurance salesman friend, a member of our church, and said he was going back into the hospital for more tests as he was not feeling well. The following Sunday I was told he was hospitalized; his kidneys and liver had ceased to function. He was in and out of a coma and his family was being called to see him for the last time.

"THERE IS VERY LITTLE WE CAN DO"

My wife and I went to the hospital that Sunday evening, and met his wife when we entered the lobby. As we stepped off the elevator her husband was being wheeled out of his room directly in front of the nurses station to another room at the very end of the corridor. It didn't dawn on me until later that he was more than likely being moved to that location because he was expected to die. The hospital would not want a large crowd of concerned family and friends gathering outside of a room in front of the nurse's station.

His wife asked the nurse tending to him what the doctor was going to do for her husband.

The nurse replied, "I don't know what the doctor is going to say, but you need to understand there is very little we can do for someone in your husband's condition."

The wife began to cry, and together we walked down the long corridor and into the room where her husband lay still and very pale. He was in a double-occupancy room and a curtain divider had been pulled separating the two beds to provide a degree of privacy. The other section was clean and spotless and obviously had been readied for a new patient.

On the other side of the curtain, seated on the edge of the bed was a large-framed man dressed in street clothes. I looked around briefly and saw he had no suitcase or personal belongings which would indicate he was a new patient. He seemed out of place, though not at all intrusive. Neither was he a friend or relative of the family. He simply sat by quietly while we proceeded to minister to our friend.

A PRAYER FOR HEALING

When we first walked into the room the wife remarked that it was the first time in a while her sick husband had been so alert and responsive. I walked to his bedside and he looked up and asked, "How are things?" I sensed he was fearful and so I reassured him there was no need to worry. We were going to pray and ask the Lord to heal him. Whether raised up out of his hospital bed or ushered into the very presence of the Lord, either way he would be made whole. There was nothing to fear.

He looked to his wife and motioned for her to come close. He expressed his love to her, wanting to make sure everything was alright between the two of them, for their marriage had been tumultuous for so long.

I placed my hand upon his chest and we prayed in agreement together for healing and peace. We expressed our love and reassurance to him and then stepped out into the corridor to speak with his wife and some Muslim friends of theirs who had arrived to comfort them as well. She asked me, "Now that we have prayed for my husband is his condition just temporary? Will he be well?" I responded by telling her, "This is what we had prayed and asked the Lord for." We then joined hands and prayed together that God would give her His peace and calm assurance.

My wife and I said good night to her and to the insurance salesman friend who remained with her at the hospital. I remarked to my wife as we walked toward the elevator that unless we had a miracle from the Lord, we would need to plan for a funeral. How's that for a positive confession from God's man of faith and power?

WHO WAS THE STRANGER?

Over the years, I have seen enough people die in hospitals to know the look of death. I suppose I was speaking more from the perspective of reality rather than a lack of faith. What a revelation of the truth *"..we do not look at the things that are seen, but at the things which are not seen"* (2Corinthians 4:18) I was about to receive!

When we reached the elevator at the end of the corridor I looked back toward our friend's room at the end of the hallway. His wife and family had vacated the corridor and obviously gone back to his bedside. It was then I noticed that the man who had been sitting quietly on the other bed stepped into the hallway, paused to look back into the room, then turned and headed down the corridor toward us.

I thought nothing of it, expecting he had business at the hospital and would possibly be stopping at the nurse's station located immediately behind us. When the elevator doors opened, this same visitor stepped onto the elevator with my wife and I and rode with us quietly to the main floor. As we vacated the elevator we paused briefly, looking for a restroom. He stepped around us and then stopped and turned to ask, "Do the two of you need assistance?"

I thanked him and told him we had located the restroom. My wife proceeded to the ladies' room not more than twenty feet down the hallway to the right of us, and the visitor turned and headed down the no-less-than 100 ft. doorless and windowless hallway to the lobby that ultimately led to the parking lot. I briefly glanced at my wife disappearing into the ladies' room, and then looked left to observe this friendly visitor continue his walk to the end of that long corridor.

To my surprise, he wasn't there! He had simply disappeared from the corridor in those three to four seconds. I tempered my confusion and wonder at what I had just experienced in order to calmly relate to my wife what I thought had just happened.

As we walked that same corridor to the lobby and parking lot, we both searched for him. The lobby was empty and the parking lot had few cars, but he was no where to be seen.

"MINISTERING SPIRITS"

In that moment the classic scriptures regarding angelic ministry came to mind. Paul testified, *"For there stood by me this night an angel of the God to whom I belong and whom I serve..."* (Acts 27:23 NKJV). David wrote, *"The angel of the Lord encamps all around those who fear Him..."* (Psalm 34:7 NKJV).

Regarding the ministry of angels, the writer of Hebrews states, *"Are not all angels ministering spirits sent to serve those who will inherit salvation?"* (Hebrews 1:14). Throughout the coming week we thought often about this visitor's presence, interaction and the unexplainable nature of his disappearance. And we told no one about it at that time.

It was a busy week for me and I hadn't heard anything further from the hospital or the family. I suspected he may have passed away, and being new believers with many friends and family who were not Christians, they may have opted for a family gathering rather than involve the church.

The following Sunday I spoke with the insurance salesman who had invited them to church and maintained a close relationship with them. I asked him about the visitor in the room who had been seated on the other bed. He said he had noticed him, but just assumed he was a worker in the hospital. I then inquired after our friend, and he said, "Oh, he may be coming home this week!"

Startled, I replied, "What do you mean?"

He told me, "Well, his kidneys are working fine and so is his liver. He's sitting up and eating."

Amazed, I asked, "What do the doctors say?"

"They don't know what to think," he happily responded.

DEATH OVERRULED!

Standing there in the sanctuary the next Sunday morning, the events of the previous week came flooding back with a renewed wonder and praise to the Lord for His power and grace to confront the forces of Hell with delivering and supernatural healing impact. I thought again of the unidentified visitor who sat quietly in the hospital room, and who joined us in the elevator and offered courteous and personal assistance to us on the main floor of the hospital. The only explanation I could give myself which made any sense in light of the circumstances, was this was something that probably happens all the time. We just aren't aware.

If the Lord does nothing in this world except by prayer and the ministry of His church, then could it be possible the Lord set an angelic guard against death in behalf of one who lay at death's door until the people of God could join together and pray the prayer of faith for healing? The Lord's plan perceptibly was to overrule death as the end result of sickness, in order to give His child the opportunity to live for Him and tell others what the Lord had done.

A few weeks later the doctors gave our friend a clean bill of health. Their unbelieving daughter, who had been called from Canada to see her father for the last time, came with an anger and resentment toward God for allowing this illness to happen—especially since her parents had just become Christians. After seeing the events unfold that week, the Holy Spirit prepared her heart to receive the witness of a

Christian friend in Canada who led her to also receive Christ.

THE WEAPON OF FEAR

Out of an arsenal of many, the greatest weapon the enemy wields is fear. It is in this *"valley of the shadow of death"* his temptations feed upon our anxiety and apprehensions. I believe most every temptation which comes our way has fear associated with it to some degree:

- We may lie for fear of being found out.
- We may steal for fear of having to miss out.
- We may cheat for fear of losing out.
- We may be promiscuous for fear of not being accepted.
- We may become addicted to the methods we use to medicate our pain for fear of not being able to cope.
- We do nothing with our lives for fear of failure.
- We end our life for fear of the future.

Fear is one of the most influential motivations in the *"valley of the shadow of death."* David stated, *"Even though I walk through the valley of the shadow of death, I will fear no evil!"*

"Fear" (yare'/Hebrew) means "dread or fright"—a paralyzing fear. *"Evil"* (ra'/Hebrew) denotes "adversity, affliction, calamity, distress, grief, hurt, mischief or sorrow."

David was declaring he would not permit the fear of adversity, hurt, mischief, sorrow, affliction or calamity to impede his walk through this *"valley of the shadow of death."*

THE PERSONAL AWARENESS OF GOD'S PRESENCE

David explained there were two reasons why he would not harbor apprehension:

First he acknowledged and was absolutely certain about the Lord's presence with him. *"For You are with me."*

The awareness of the Lord can be felt by the human soul. David knew something of this presence through subjective experiences. It was something he had personally felt in the past.

When facing Goliath, David contributed his past victories over a lion and a bear to the presence and power of the Lord he had known. *"Your servant has killed both the lion and the bear; this uncircumcised Philistine will be like one of them, because he has defied the armies of the living God. The LORD who delivered me from the paw of the lion and the paw of the bear will deliver me from the hand of this Philistine. Saul said to David, 'Go, and the LORD be with you'"* (1 Samuel 17:36-37).

David had encounters with God, and this is one reason why even though in *"the valley of the shadow of death"* he would not fear.

The Holy Spirit, which was the presence and power of the Lord for David to experience, is the same Holy Spirit today. Pentecostal and Charismatic Christian believers know something about this dimension in their walk with the Lord. However, I have always warned to beware of anyone manifesting "gifts of the Spirit" (1 Corinthians 12:1-10) and not the "fruit of the Spirit" (Galatians 5:22-23; Ephesians 5:9) in their life.

Neither accept as valid a Christian's claim to having a spiritual gift(s) when they refuse to walk in right relationship with others. They may be "manifesting" something but it won't be a gift from the Holy Spirit!

Scripture is very clear concerning those gifts flowing in love and for the edification and building up of the church (1 Corinthians 12-13).

A gentleman took me to lunch one day and told me he had a "special gift" from the Lord. In fact his mother confirmed it to him as a boy growing up. He said he "knows" things. And yet he was a man who walked in division, strife, prideful arrogance, disrespect for authority, criticism and control.

He had a "gift" alright, but the "lord" he received it from wasn't from the Lord Jesus. And the spirit which motivated him was not characteristic of the person of the Holy Spirit.

Subjective spiritual experience is not the validation for truth. But truth can and will be subjectively experienced. Why? Because truth is not just a theological system or moral code of ethics we attempt to live. Truth is a person. And Jesus is the only One who laid absolute claims to such a title. He said *"I am the way, the truth and the life"* (John 14:6).

David, as an Old Testament believer enjoyed God's presence empowering his life again and again. His anointing with oil by Samuel the priest for the office of king in Israel was the visible symbol of the unseen anointing presence of God upon David for his life and leadership role (1 Samuel 16:13). His music was a manifestation of the presence of God operating in revelation knowledge and prophetic song.

If you are going to walk through *"the valley of the shadow of death"* and *"fear no evil,"* you will need to know something about subjectively experiencing the presence of God in the fullness of His Spirit. We don't seek signs and wonders for they can lie, depending upon their source (2 Thessalonians 2:9-10). But signs, wonders and encounters with the presence of the Lord are legitimate personal evidences the soul can receive. They serve to change us and to make the Lord real to our hearts and minds. David knew God was with him for he had experienced His presence in circumstantial encounters.

THE WRITTEN AND THE LIVING WORD
Second, David knew something of what to expect from God.
He had the Word which brought support for believing, instruction for living and directive for praying and battling. David said, *"Your rod and staff they comfort me."* "Rod" (shebet/Hebrew) means "stick for correction, fighting, or a scepter signifying authority."

The "shebet" of God's Word is the sword of the Spirit (Ephesians 6:17). It contains the authoritative promises of the Almighty which I can use against all the plans and attacks of my spiritual enemy. The "shebet" of the Word is the standard of truth (2 Timothy 3:16) I need to bring correction to my own heart's desire. It contains the Lord's instruction to my personal intellect about right living. It gives His guidance to my own plans for life. But this Word is a living Word because it is the Word of a living God. He is the eternal Word that *"became flesh and dwelt among us"* (John 1:14).

Jesus declares, *"The words that I speak to you they are spirit and they are life"* (John 6:63 NKJV). This means He is present in His Word to communicate it with freshness and revelation to your spirit.

The prophesies of the Messiah addressed Him as "The Scepter." *"The Scepter shall not depart from Judah, Nor a lawgiver from between his feet, until Shiloh comes; And to Him shall be the obedience of the people"* (Genesis 49:10 NKJV). *"A Star shall come out of Jacob; A Scepter shall rise out of Israel"* (Numbers 24:17 NKJV).

Jesus tells us authority was His *"to execute judgment"* (John.5:27). He stated, *"All authority has been given to Me in heaven and on earth"* (Matthew 28:18 NKJV). Prayer in His name through faith in His Word touches the "Scepter" of His authority and releases His miracle-working power.

The Holy Spirit was careful to include both terms *"rod"* and *"staff"* to give us the complete picture of the Word of God bringing comfort. *"Staff"* (mishena/Hebrew) literally means a "walking stick." It is figurative of support and sustenance for the journey. *"Comfort"* (nacham/Hebrew) is translated "consolation, to bring a sigh of relief."

It was the Word of God which encouraged, reassured, sustained and strengthened David in His trek through this *"valley of the shadow of death."* The revelation of the Father's grace brought a sigh of relief to his soul in every personal failure. And the promise of God's presence and power brought the same relief in every challenge he faced.

In Psalm 119 David repeats this theme of support, sustenance and comfort which the Word of the Lord brought to His life (NKJV):

> *"And I will walk at liberty, for I seek Your precepts"* (Psalm 119:45).
> *"This is my comfort in my affliction, for Your word has given me life"* (v.50).
> *"Your statutes have been my songs In the house of my*

pilgrimage" (v.54).

"I will never forget Your precepts, for by them You have given me life" (v.93).

"Your word is a lamp to my feet and a light to my path" (v.105).

"The entrance of Your words gives light; It gives understanding to the simple" (v.130).

"Direct my steps by Your word, and let no iniquity have dominion over me" (v.133).

"Great peace have those who love Your law, and nothing causes them to stumble" (v.165).

Because God was a God of His Word, David knew something of what to expect from the Lord.

The power to confront the forces of Hell is found in life-changing, soul-strengthening, spirit-invigorating encounters with the presence of the Holy Spirit. These encounters with the Lord are determined by the promise of God in His Word, the sovereign work of the Almighty in our life, and the true motive and condition of our heart.

In the New Testament, Peter encouraged the early believers to expect visitations of God's Spirit if they would meet the conditions. *"Repent, then, and turn to God, so that your sins may be wiped out, that times of refreshing may come from the Lord"* (Acts 3:19). James counseled, *"Come near to God and He will come near to you. Wash your hands, you sinners, and purify your hearts, you double-minded"* (James 4:8). And Jesus made this promise: *"But you will receive power when the Holy Spirit comes on you; and you will be My witnesses in Jerusalem, and in all Judea and Samaria, and to the ends of the earth"* (Acts 1:8). *"And these signs will accompany those who believe: In my name they will drive out demons; they will speak in new tongues...they will place their hands on sick people, and they will get well"* (Mark 16:17-18).

———— ⚬━⨡⧚⧚⧚⌐ ————

The power to confront the forces of Hell is also
found when by prayer and a lifestyle of faith and obedience,
we press claims upon the promises of God's Word and
walk forward in an offensive strategy.

Confrontation is not a defensive stance, rather an *offensive* one. Since Christ's victory over sin at the Cross, His utter defeat of death and Hell at His resurrection and His delegation of authority by His Spirit outpoured on the Day of Pentecost, we are on the attack, not the defensive, when it comes to the forces of Hell. We are the intimidators, not the intimidated. We are enforcers of Christ's victorious confrontation. *"We are more than conquerors through Him who loved us"* (Romans 8:37).

Long before it was captured as a popular slogan and screened onto a T-shirt, "NO FEAR" was David's God-given position and disposition in his walk through this *"valley of the shadow of death."*

It is also ours!

CHAPTER NINE

FINDING MORAL AND SPIRITUAL FORTITUDE

*"You prepare a table before me in the presence of my enemies.
You anoint my head with oil; my cup overflows."*
– PSALM 23:5

As David wrote of God's provision for him in the presence of his enemies, it was more than just picture words. The reality was, David had enemies—who wanted him dead!

The battle was both spiritual and human in nature. The threats against his life were very real in the natural realm, inspired by adversaries in the spirit realm that stood in opposition to the plan of God for David's life. All of our conflicts as Christians are spiritually inspired, and most of them are pressed in the realm of human relationships. For these battles we need the moral and spiritual fortitude the Holy Spirit gives to us as the power of our right response in any given situation.

A SPIRITUAL ENEMY;
A HUMAN BATTLEGROUND

The Bible is clear that what really rules our course is the condition of our spiritual life. Before we receive Christ our human spirit is "dead"—unresponsive to God—and our sin nature has dominion.

My "spiritual life" is the relationship I have with the Lord Jesus Christ who's Holy Spirit indwells and rules me through my human spirit. According to John 3:3-8 when I am "born again of the Spirit" it is my human spirit which now comes alive to God to experience communion, fellowship and revelation from the Spirit of God.

When the Lord speaks to me it is by His Holy Spirit to my human spirit. Paul describes the vitality of our Christian walk as being *"fervent in spirit serving the Lord"* (Romans12:11 NKJV). He also portrays our relationship as being, *"He who is joined to the Lord is one spirit with Him"* (1 Corinthians 6:17 NKJV).

If this divine alliance is strong and vital, then the Holy Spirit exerts a governing influence over my human spirit and impacts my thinking and my emotions. He overrules my wrong, negative, destructive feelings and thinking process which is contrary to the Word of God. The Bible is also clear that our real enemies are spiritual in nature. *"For we do not wrestle against flesh and blood, but against principalities, against powers, against the rulers of the darkness of this age, against spiritual hosts of wickedness in the heavenly places"* (Ephesians 6:12 NKJV).

The word David used for *"enemies"* (tsarar/Hebrew) denotes literally "to cramp." By application then, enemies are those whose influence upon our souls and spirits is to "bind, distress, oppress, shut up or force into a narrow place." Some people have that kind of affect on us. There are individuals whose association tends to hold us back, drag us down to their level, constrict our creativity and Kingdom life potential and throw a shroud over a faith-filled outlook.

If this is the affect and sway some exert upon you by their words, actions and attitudes, they don't love you. And if they don't love you they do not have a right to speak into your life.

The devil works by the power of suggestion to make our circumstances have the same affect. By planting deceitful seeds of doubt, our spiritual enemy capitalizes upon our circumstances, people's words and actions, events, our emotions, human thinking and perspective and our own limited understanding of things to force our spirit into a narrow place in order to bind us, oppress and shut us up in distress, unbelief and defeat.

_The work of our spiritual enemy is to constrict our spirit
into the narrow place of being ruled by our emotions and
our own thinking rather than the Spirit of God. He seeks
to keep us living on a "reactive" level of doubt and fear
rather than a "proactive" level of faith in God._

When your spiritual enemy is able to achieve this, he can famish, starve, diminish and malnourish your spirit, rendering it weak in obedience to the Holy Spirit. The purpose is so your emotions will rule your life rather than the Holy Spirit. And your prideful thoughts or human reasoning takes charge rather than the Word of God. _"For those who live according to the flesh set their minds on the things of the flesh, but those who live according to the Spirit, the things of the Spirit. For to be carnally minded is death, but to be spiritually minded is life and peace"_ (Romans 8:5-6 NKJV).

The reason this battle rages so furious at times is because the devil is often more cognizant of what your life can mean for Christ's Kingdom than you are.

RELEVANT KINGDOM LIVING

The Cross is proof that every individual is important to God, and so was David. Unfortunately, because of the choices people make here on earth, many do not build God's Kingdom.

I attended a denominational gathering of ministers a number of years ago in eastern Washington where Dr. Lloyd Ogilvie was our guest speaker for the weekend. One of the statements I remember him making resonated within me and has remained in my mind ever since. In speaking to church and denominational leadership he felt prompted to challenge us to reach the lost. This may not be a verbatim quote, but here is the essence of what he said: "If you haven't personally shared the Gospel with an unbeliever in the past thirty days you are _irreverent_ to Christ. If you haven't won someone to the Lord in the past six moths you are _irrelevant_ to the Kingdom work of Christ."

David mattered greatly to the Kingdom of God for two reasons. First, because of the Lord's sovereign call upon his life. And second, because of his "heart attitude" toward God. It takes both to be a threat to the kingdom of darkness and a champion for the Kingdom.

The Lord's call upon each of us will be realized only as far as we respond rightly to Him. Whatever God's calling, to respond in faith and obedience in pursuit of it will set off alarms in hell. You're going to discover enemies you never thought you had. For David they included those of his own household.

In speaking for the Lord, Samuel the priest pointed out the characteristic of David which God found attractive. *"The Lord has sought out a man after His own heart"* (1 Samuel 13:14). The Living Bible's translation states, *"The Lord wants a man who will obey Him"* The word *"heart"* (lebab/Hebrews) refers to "the inner man; the inclinations, resolutions, determinations of the will; the center of emotions, appetites and passions of the heart; the thought processes of the intellect."

AN ETERNAL PURPOSE

This quality of obedience from the heart is the key to finding moral and spiritual fortitude. David was an imperfect man with the same struggles which are common to every individual. He was a sinner who paid the price for his transgressions in his personal and family life. But most important, his response to God was always right.

David's deepest passion and desire was to draw near to the Almighty and glorify Him. His inner man "hooked up" with the heart of the Father in prayerful fellowship, worship and praise, and his songs reflect that. He felt the heartbeat of God's desire in his own heart.

His times alone with the Lord moved him with great emotion, and his greatest intellectual pursuit was to know the Word and the ways of God. The Father's values and priorities communicated in His Word became David's as well.

His reverence for the Lord brought to him a wisdom *from* God and knowledge *of* God which made an indelible mark upon his son Solomon. So much so that when he was anointed kingly successor to the throne of his father, wisdom is all Solomon requested from the

Lord. God granted his desire and, *"The whole world sought audience with Solomon to hear the wisdom God had put in his heart"* (1 Kings 10:24). His will was ever ready to be subservient to the will of God because he understood his kingdom and throne really weren't his. They were a gift from the Lord for which he was accountable as a steward.

The promises God made to David went beyond the scope of his days on earth. They included the coming eternal kingdom and throne of the Messiah and King of Heaven. By making God's will his, David served to bring to pass eternal purposes grander than anything else his life could ever accomplish. For these reasons David had mortal enemies.

THE POWER OF A RIGHT RESPONSE

Opposition comes because we are living to do what we understand to be God's will. For this reason moral and spiritual fortitude is needed the most. Help is sent to us from the Holy Spirit, *"strengthening us with power in our inner being"* (Ephesians 3:16). And it is released to us as the power of a right response.

———————

Moral and spiritual fortitude is given when we make the choice to respond in a way that is honoring to God and obedient to His Word and the prompting of the Holy Spirit.

There are a number of incidents in David's life when individuals took an adversarial position against him. These illustrate the Lord's shepherding influence. The power of his right response brought a release of moral and spiritual strength from the Holy Spirit.

The first was David's response to king Saul when he had the chance to kill him in the cave where David was hiding, and where Saul just so happened to lodge for the night. A spirit of revenge and prideful ambition came to tempt David in this personal battle.

Although his military experts advised him to end Saul's life and take it as God's gift, David knew this was not the issue. His word to

Saul was, *"This day you have seen with your own eyes how the LORD delivered you into my hands in the cave. Some urged me to kill you, but I spared you; I said, 'I will not lift my hand against my master, because he is the LORD's anointed.' See, my father, look at this piece of your robe in my hand! I cut off the corner of your robe but did not kill you. Now understand and recognize that I am not guilty of wrongdoing or rebellion. I have not wronged you, but you are hunting me down to take my life. May the LORD judge between you and me. And may the LORD avenge the wrongs you have done to me, but my hand will not touch you"* (1 Samuel 24:10-13).

David understood the matter was greater than whether or not Saul left the cave alive. The issue was that the kingdom of Israel was not his for the taking. It was God's for the giving. Therefore he asked for the Lord to do the judging, not himself.

David chose to allow the kingdom promised to him to be God's gift placed in his hand, not something taken by his hand. This decision released moral and spiritual fortitude in David's life and served to further qualify him for his rule in Israel.

A CHOICE FOR DAVID

The second instance is found in 2 Samuel 16. David was running from Absalom, fleeing for his safety. His son had led an uprising against him and Absalom had temporarily usurped the throne in Israel. In some ways David was now reaping the fruit of his immorality and the consequential loss of influence in his own family.

Absalom was a handsome, charming and yet undisciplined young man. He had grown up in the palace, yet his heart had filled with disrespect for his father, rebellion toward God and covetousness toward the throne. And so he plotted to kill his father to obtain what he wanted.

There was probably no lower time in David's existence than this period of running and hiding from his own son and those who had conspired with Absalom against him.

If you have ever suffered loss and those of your own household have been your greatest critics through the ordeal, you may be able to identify with David in a measured way. His story is certainly a lesson to all of us concerning moral and spiritual courage which is released by the Holy Spirit because of the power of a right response.

The Bible gives the following detailed record of this account *"As King David approached Bahurim, a man from the same clan as Saul's family came out from there. His name was Shimei son of Gera, and he cursed as he came out. He pelted David and all the king's officials with stones, though all the troops and the special guard were on David's right and left. As he cursed, Shimei said, 'Get out, get out, you man of blood, you scoundrel! The LORD has repaid you for all the blood you shed in the household of Saul, in whose place you have reigned. The LORD has handed the kingdom over to your son Absalom. You have come to ruin because you are a man of blood!' Then Abishai son of Zeruiah said to the king, 'Why should this dead dog curse my lord the king? Let me go over and cut off his head'"* (2 Samuel 16:5-9).

Don't you just love a guy like Abishai? I have always believed that every senior pastor needs at least one board member just like him!

"But the king said, 'What do you and I have in common, you sons of Zeruiah? If he is cursing because the LORD said to him, "Curse David," who can ask, "Why do you do this?" David then said to Abishai and all his officials, 'My son, who is of my own flesh, is trying to take my life. How much more, then, this Benjamite! Leave him alone; let him curse, for the LORD has told him to. It may be that the LORD will see my distress and repay me with good for the cursing I am receiving today'" (vv.10-12).

THE FINAL JUDGE

A spirit of hatred aroused hostile criticism from Abishei and a murderous spirit inciting self-vindication came to tempt David. Although the Biblical narrative doesn't go into much detail concerning what went into David's decision-making process, it was a very real temptation for David to end Shimei's life because of the cursing attack, particularly at this very low ebb in his life.

As king in Israel, David had both the power and the privilege to do so. The might of the king was autonomous and his judgment final. David didn't even have to commit the killing personally or command Shimei's beheading. Abishai was more than ready to do the ten-second job right then and there! All David would have had to do was to look the other way and just refuse to restrain Abishai, and it would have all been over. But David knew God was also in this encounter with Shimei. He understood that to kill this man would place him on the same level as Absalom who was seeking his life.

This was both a test and an opportunity for the Holy Spirit to grant moral and spiritual fortitude through the power of a right response.

God knew if He could shepherd David in this powerful and personal affront, than it would truly be God who ruled as the unseen King in Israel once David was restored to the throne.

The Lord was securing a man who would allow Him to be King in Israel, ruling from the throne of David's heart. Because the Lord was shepherding his life, David refused to act on the power and privilege of position without the right before God to do so. His willingness to allow the Lord to be the final judge of Shimei's actions released the spiritual and moral fortitude he needed to call off his loyal and zealous "head-hunter," Abishei.

THE INSANITY OF SIN

David's affair with Bathsheba and his role in the death of her husband Uriah was also a reference point from which David could recall the tragic results of exercising the power and privilege of position without the moral or spiritual right to do so. Even though David took the widow Bathsheba as his spouse, God never referred to her as David's wife. She is always spoken of in Scripture as the wife of Uriah. David had come to understand that the privilege of king over Israel was not synonymous with personal rights before God.

So David refused to make a "dead dog" out of the "barking dog" Shimei. David spared his life and allowed the Lord, not himself, to be the final judge of this man. The actions by Shimei, cursing and pelting the king of Israel and his mighty military men with dirt and stones, is totally absurd when you consider that Abishei had to know that his life and future were at risk.

Sin never makes sense. In fact, it is insanity. It serves as a lesson to us that our own adversarial critics only emulate in their words and actions the foolishness which is characteristic of all sinful behavior.

If the Lord is shepherding your life it will never be more than hateful ranting. In fact David viewed it as an opportunity to experience the blessing of the Lord as the result of his right response. *"It may be that the LORD will see my distress and repay me with good for the cursing I am receiving today"* (2 Samuel 16:10).

LET THE LORD REPAY

David's reaction was much like another of God's great champions, A. B. Simpson, who said, *"I solemnly believe that most of my blessings in life and ministry come from the evil things people say about me, because God makes me willing to allow them to do it."*

We know the outcome of the ordeal for David was that he was restored to the throne. But what about Shimei? After the death of Absalom, Shimei came groveling before David begging for mercy—which David granted. After the death of David, king Solomon insisted that Shimei be restricted to his land, living under a kind of "house arrest." However, because of his defiance of Solomon's order he was put to death.

The Biblical record is as follows. *"The king also said to Shimei, 'You know in your heart all the wrong you did to my father David. Now the LORD will repay you for your wrongdoing. But King Solomon will be blessed, and David's throne will remain secure before the LORD forever.' Then the king gave the order to Benaiah son of Jehoiada, and he went out and struck Shimei down and killed him"* (1 Kings 2:44-46).

THE ARK OF GOD

A third instance is found in 2 Samuel chapters five and six. *"David knew that the LORD had established him as king over Israel and had exalted his kingdom for the sake of his people Israel"* (2 Samuel 5:12).

David's leadership had united the kingdom of Israel. However, David the song writer, singer and praise leader, who's head was still spinning with unprecedented military victories, the acquisition of many new concubines and wives, a growing family (v.13), and the construction of a new home as a gift from Hiram, the king of Tyre (vv.11-12), had to learn that the time of God's abundant blessing can bring with it the temptation to walk in gross presumption.

After a number of military victories over the Philistines which brought peace and security to the land, David focused attention upon the true treasure of his heart, which was the ark of God. *"David again brought together out of Israel chosen men, thirty thousand in all. He and all his men set out from Baalah of Judah to bring up from there the ark of God, which is called by the Name, the name of the LORD Almighty, who is enthroned between the cherubim that are on the ark"* (2 Samuel 6:1-2).

"HANDLING" GOD'S PRESENCE

David was a worshiper. He desired closeness with God and the Lord's promised presence resided with the ark. 2 Samuel chapter six records how David planned a grand processional of celebrative music and dance to bring and welcome the ark to Jerusalem. The ark was carried on a new cart pulled by oxen. After the extravagant production ended in fiasco with the death of Uzzah, David's pride was injured and he was both displeased with God and fearful of Him. So he stashed the ark in the home of Obed-edom.

When word spread that the household of Obed-edom was blessed in every way because of the presence of the ark, David realized as never before that it is important how you "handle" the presence of the Lord. King David needed a reminder that it doesn't matter how marvelous your choir and dance team is, if you don't reverence His presence.

Bringing the ark to Jerusalem was attempted a second time. On this journey it was carried on the shoulders of the priests in the manner God had prescribed. It was a signal the Lord wanted to be near to His people. The ostentatious display of artistic and musical talent was replaced by sacrificial offerings every eighteen feet, shouts of praise and the sounding of the trumpet.

When the ark finally reached its destination and the processional participants had also made it unscathed, David's sense of God's favor and presence so overwhelmed him that he worshiped in reckless abandon and danced publicly with all his might. He did so having cast off the outer layers of his royal garments.

Unwittingly, David was demonstrating that whether you're the king, a peasant or an angel is immaterial. We are all on the same plane when we praise and worship before the Lord.

When the ark was set in place, David offered burnt and peace offerings to the Lord and blessed the people. All in Jerusalem were given bread, meat and wine to take home and feast upon. When David arrived home he was confronted by his wife Michal who viewed David's dance of praise with disgust and embarrassment. The Bible says she *"despised him in her heart"* (2 Samuel 6:16) *"When David returned home to bless his household, Michal daughter of Saul came out to meet him and said, 'How the king of Israel has distinguished himself today, disrobing in the sight of the slave girls of his servants as any vulgar fellow would!' David said to Michal, 'It was before the LORD, who chose me rather than your father or anyone from his house when He appointed me ruler over the LORD's people Israel—I will celebrate before the LORD. I will become even more undignified than this, and I will be humiliated in my own eyes. But by these slave girls you spoke of, I will be held in honor.' And Michal daughter of Saul had no children to the day of her death"* (2 Samuel 6:20-23).

Through Michal's reaction, a "religious spirit" came to quench

David's passionate praise and worship of God and subjugate it to a more humanly acceptable, predictable, prescribed form. This is what a religious spirit always seeks to do.

———————— ❦ ————————

David's response of humility released the moral and spiritual fortitude he needed as a leader to confront a religious spirit of prideful formalism which sought to quench spiritual fervor for God among the people.

When David finished his outward expression of spontaneous praise, the word in the kingdom wasn't "What a great dancer David is!" The lasting impression of such a celebration became, "What a great God we have among us!"

GOD PREPARES A TABLE

The fruit of David's spontaneity, humility and fervency of praise and worship to the Lord amounted to literally millions of dollars worth of materials given by the people and gathered for the marvelous wonder of the temple of Solomon—which was built for worship to the Lord. Praise and worship made the building project the passion and purpose of David's life. And it sparked a spiritual fervor which made the temple truly a place the Spirit of God inhabited after it had been built (1 Kings 8:1-11).

On the other hand, the fruit of a religious spirit is illustrated in the barrenness of Michal's womb. The Bible doesn't say God cursed Michal with no children. Her inability to conceive may have been the result of David knowing she despised him in her heart and so he would have nothing more to do with her.

This may not be the way to treat a wife in the 21st century, and especially in western culture, but it's the only way to treat a spirit of religion if your going to maintain a fervent, humble, spirit of spontaneous praise which is obedient to the moving of the Holy Spirit upon your heart.

Sometimes leadership wins the battle against a religious spirit in the church as David did that day. At other times leadership loses such a battle.

When this happens, everybody loses. A religious spirit replaces heart-felt spontaneity with religious exercise—and this form is mistaken for spiritual reality.

In the presence of my spiritual enemies, who try to *"diminish, cramp, shut up, force into a narrow place, or oppress"* my life in the Spirit, God prepares a table, and He spreads before me a meal to nourish my spirit, and the menu includes three things:

1: The Word of God.

Jeremiah said, *"Your words were found, and I ate them. And Your word was to me the joy and rejoicing of my heart"* (Jeremiah 15:16 NKJV). And Jesus declared, *"The words that I have spoken to you are spirit and they are life"* (John 6:63).

The powerful Word of God has impact and influence upon my spirit. The word *"life"* (zoe/Greek) here means "fullness, purpose, and destiny." It is life as God would live it. The Word communicates and imparts "zoe," which is the *"absolute fullness that belongs to God"* to your human spirit by the ministry of the indwelling Holy Spirit.

David was continually nourished by the Word of the Lord and the prophetic promises God had made to him. It is what gave him the power to respond rightly in challenging situations. David wrote, *"I have hidden your Word in my heart that I might not sin against You"* (Psalm 119:11).

Confusion, doubt, double-mindedness and compromise are the signs of a human spirit which is starving for the nourishment of life-giving truth only the Word of God can bring. It is part of the banqueting table the Lord spreads for us in the presence of our enemies.

2: The Spirit of God.

The Holy Spirit is the person of the Godhead who is the literal presence and power of God at work in this world and in every follower of Jesus. He is present to convict mankind of sin, righteousness and judgment (John 16:8), to make the Christian like

Jesus (v.15), to enlighten and reveal the Word of God to the human understanding (1 Corinthians 2:9-16) and to empower the Church to carry on the ministry of Jesus (John 14:12).

The Bible declares it is by the gifts of the Holy Spirit that Jesus carries on in ministry through His church (Romans12; Ephesians 4; 1 Corinthians 12). It was the Spirit of God which moved upon David to write a worship song, as well as endowing him with strength to kill the lion, the bear and the giant Goliath.

The Holy Spirit moved in conviction to bring him to true repentance, and with wisdom to battle, build and lead Israel into its greatest period of peace and prosperity. Powerlessness, prayerlessness, lack of ministry, ineffectiveness in witness and prideful offense at the manifestation of the Spirit's gifts, are signs a human spirit is famished for the nourishment that the Holy Spirit alone can give. No matter what you have experienced of the precious and powerful ministry of the Holy Spirit, there is always more!

3: The People of God.

The Lord sent individuals into David's life to strengthen and encourage him. Saul's own son, Jonathan was a God-given friend who walked with him through the madness of his father's unrelenting pursuit, intent on David's destruction. The love and loyalty of David's mighty military men kept him safe and his hope alive.

The Word of God tells us how we are to relate to each another and the ministry we share with one another.

- *"Love one another"* (John15:12 NKJV).
- *"Be kindly affectionate and devoted to one another"* (Romans 12:10 NKJV).
- *"Let us not judge one another"* (Romans14:13 NAS).
- *"Receive one another"* (Romans 15:17 NKJV).
- *"Serve one another"* (Galatians 5:13 NKJV).
- *"...bearing with one another, and forgiving one another"* (Colossians 3:13 NKJV).
- *"Comfort one another"* (1 Thessalonians 4:18 NKJV).
- *"Build each other up"* (1 Thessalonians 5:11 ASV).

- *"Encourage one another"* (Hebrews 3:13).
- *"Stimulate one another to love and good deeds"* (Hebrews 10:24 NAS).

The Word of God warns of the consequences of not relating rightly to others:

- We hurt people and destroy friendships. *"If you are critical and catty, and keep biting and devouring one another, you will be destroyed by each other"* (Galatians 5:15 TLB).
- We live hypocritically and make a sham of Christian fellowship. *"If someone says, 'I love God,' and hates his brother, he is a liar; for he who does not love his brother whom he has seen, how can he love God whom he has not seen?"* (1 John 4:20 NKJV).
- Our worship and ministry is rejected by God. *"If you are offering your gift at the altar and there remember that your brother has something against you, leave your gift there in front of the altar. First go and be reconciled to your brother; then come and offer your gift"* (Matthew 5:23-24).
- Our witness to the world is invalidated. *"By this all will know that you are My disciples, if you have love for one another"* (John 13:35 NKJV).

Strife, criticism, arrogant independence, disloyalty, aloofness, cold disaffection, hurt-nursing and pain-rehearsing are signs of a human spirit which is starving for the nourishment that loving fellowship with God's people alone can give—but unforgiveness separates them from this blessing.

The Lord spreads the table before us in the presence of our enemies so our spiritual life can be sustained. Yet He doesn't force-feed anyone. I must willingly partake of the Word of God and open my heart to the fullness of the Spirit of God. I must also commit to fellowship with believers.

THE FOUNDATION FOR PERSONAL MINISTRY

The last two statements David makes in this passage speak to us concerning the results of partaking of the table the Lord spreads before us. David said, *"You anoint my head with oil."*

It is not only the picture of being refreshed before dinner, it represents that the anointing of the Holy Spirit for ministry to others comes from a heaven-fed spiritual life.

You and I cannot share the Lord with others out of a famished spirit, and God won't anoint our fleshly attempts. David had been anointed for His kingly role in Israel and the oil had been poured over his head as a sign of God's calling and the Holy Spirit's enabling for the task.

Saul was rejected as King before David because of a malnourished spirit which brought him into personal and public ruin. On the other hand, David proclaimed, "My cup overflows."

Out of a nurtured spirit not only flows ministry to others, but acceptable ministry to the Lord in worship and praise.

- A nourished spirit finds a way to praise the Lord through any song that's chosen, no matter who is leading.
- A nourished spirit can't sit with its hands folded and pout about the music style when the shout of the King's presence is among God's worshiping people.
- A nourished spirit can't help but spill out onto others a testimony of the goodness of God even in the worst of times.
- A nourished spirit won't hold back it's sacrificial gift when there are needs to be met and open doors of ministry for the Lord the church must walk through.
- A nourished spirit shows upon the face with a turned-up smile not a turned-up nose and a furrowed brow.
- A nourished spirit puts an arm around people; encourages, loves and lifts them up in prayer no matter what they look or smell like.
- A nourished spirit rightly discerns the body of Christ and makes commitments to fellowship and ministry which

are not dependant upon how good one feels concerning everything in the church.

■ A nourished spirit is led by the Holy Spirit and evidences a supernatural authority and authenticity in ministry to others.

■ A nourished spirit makes Jesus attractive to people who don't know Him.

■ A nourished spirit doesn't live in lack. It lives life in the overflow of God's blessing, provision, prosperity and favor.

When the Lord shepherds my life, I enjoy food which nourishes and sustains my spiritual being. For He *"prepares for me a table in the presence of my enemies."* He *"anoints my head with oil. My cup overflows."* And I find spiritual and moral fortitude from the Holy Spirit through the power of a right response.

CHAPTER TEN

FINDING GOD'S
GOODNESS AND
MERCY

*"Surely goodness and mercy shall follow me all the days of my
life; And I will dwell in the house of the Lord forever."*
– PSALM 23:6 NKJV

W hen the Lord shepherds my life, the events of my journey
are ultimately displays of God's goodness and mercy.

The longer I live, the farther the backward glance—and when I
take the time to look I will see these displayed in the outcome of
events, relationships, provision, blessing and safe-keeping.

David testified to this truth when he wrote, *"LORD, You have
assigned me my portion and my cup. You have made my lot secure.
The boundary lines have fallen for me in pleasant places; surely I
have a delightful inheritance"* (Psalm 16:5-6).

His life was no "ride on a pink duck." David walked through some
miserable events, and he had the same enemies which leadership in
every generation has; those who paint a bulls-eye on your back just
because you're anointed and appointed by God to be the servant "in
charge."

He experienced the personal tragedy and failure which is
associated with adultery and murder. And one outcome was God's
denial of David's greatest life passion, to build a temple in Israel for
the Lord. Scripture records, *"David rose to his feet and said: 'Listen*

155

to me, my brothers and my people. I had it in my heart to build a house as a place of rest for the ark of the covenant of the LORD, for the footstool of our God, and I made plans to build it. But God said to me', 'You are not to build a house for My Name, because you are a warrior and have shed blood'" (1 Chronicles 28:2-3).

Granted, David's mission in Israel had been a preparatory one of battle and conquest. In contrast, the Messiah's reign over the nations of the world will be as the "Prince of Peace." So in this sense the characteristic of David's rule would not so fitly represent the peaceful reign of the Messiah that will yet occur from the temple in Jerusalem.

Even though it isn't specifically mentioned by David here, his battle campaigns included the pre-arranged death of his commander Uriah. And that was the shedding of innocent blood. So when David speaks of his past in terms of *"pleasant places"* he wasn't just putting a positive spin on regret and tragedy. Rather, David acknowledges God didn't deal with him the way he deserved. *"He does not treat us as our sins deserve or repay us according to our iniquities"* (Psalm 103:10).

David's prayer for God's goodness and mercy had been answered. *"Do not remember the sins of my youth, nor my transgressions; According to Your mercy remember me, For Your goodness' sake, O LORD"* (Psalm 25:7 NKJV). The backward glance revealed that through it all, in spite of it all— and for the purpose of displaying to all—God had constructed a framework of goodness and established boundaries of mercy in which he could clearly rejoice. It gave him cause to hope for the future. *"Surely I have a delightful inheritance"* (Psalm 16:6).

OUR FAILURES AND THE GOODNESS AND MERCY OF GOD

God's grace and compassion "following us" means that's how He deals with our past when we allow Him to shepherd our life. David is looking at his yesterdays, the panorama of his past. His memory wanders back and walks him through the path of his spent years.

God has given us a memory, and when illness does not render it weak, it serves this purpose very well. It is true that for every individual who is burdened with fears of tomorrow, there are many who are weighed down with the hurt and regret of yesterday.

A burdened conscience never comes from tomorrow, it surfaces from our past.

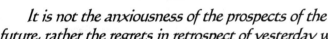

It is not the anxiousness of the prospects of the future, rather the regrets in retrospect of yesterday which can oppress our mind, depress our soul and lay the heaviest weight upon our hearts.

David could recall his life and see it illustrated somewhat in the mirror image of a slug leaving a slime trail everywhere it has been. On his own, his life—like ours—doesn't leave much more of a trace for eternal good and glory than that of a lowly slug.

Mixed with the victories and glories of His leadership of Israel and his walk with God, were events of sinful failure, fear and compromise. Deep hurt was the result. David's failures were always related to the fact he failed to consult the Lord regarding His will, and then would stop trusting Him and take matters into his own hands.

For example, even though God had demonstrated supernatural intervention to protect David from those who came from Saul to arrest him (1 Samuel 19), in fear for his safety David ran from Saul, scheming and lying in order to steal holy bread out of the tabernacle from the Priest Ahimelech. He also acted like an insane person before King Achish of Gath to save his life and hide in the cave of Adullam. (1Samuuel 21).

THE FALLOUT FROM STRESS

David's greatest failures followed periods of extreme success and popularity. In 2 Samuel 24, David had been admonished by Joab, his military commander-in-chief, that he had no right to rejoice in their military strength. And yet David insisted upon taking a census of his army. He demonstrated a prideful independence and lack of trust in God to give the victory.

Though David's conscience bothered him and he repented, the result was a three-day plague from the Lord which killed 70,000 people in Israel. 2 Samuel 11-12 records that when David was in his 20-year cycle of military prowess and prosperity as king of Israel, and when he should have accompanied his army in military exercises, he remained in the leisure of the palace in Jerusalem. This gave birth to sin's opportunity of adultery with Bathseba and a murderous conspiracy to do away with her husband. The fallout from stress and anxiety plagued him and his family the rest of his days.

In many ways, this disqualified David from correcting and disciplining his own children when they committed the same sins. At times, David misinterpreted his success and popularity as a sign of God's blanket approval on all he was doing. His talents, gifts and prosperity were indeed a blessing from God, but he failed to realize such success is not necessarily a measurement of spiritual maturity or present rightness with the Lord. Sometimes it is God's goodness which is meant to lead us to repentance (Romans 2:4).

The continual prayer of David was, *"Keep back Your servant also from presumptuous sins; Let them not have dominion over me"* (Psalm 19:13 NKJV). Each time he acknowledged his transgressions and truly repented, God forgave and restored him to fellowship with Himself. *"Mercy and goodness"* followed him all the days of his life and wiped away the slime trail.

Like the sands of a pristine beach which have been marred by foot traffic, raucous activity and littered with trash, the tide of God's ""goodness and mercy" had swept in and left the sands of his life clean and smooth once again.

When you look back, do you become depressed at the trail you are leaving? Only when the Lord shepherds your life is there an answer for such regret.

WHAT FOLLOWS US?

Thank God it isn't "justice shall follow me all the days of my life" or some of us would be locked up in a prison cell this very moment. Or maybe we'd be divorced for the third time and the person we are now living with refuses to marry us! We could be in a hospital dying from a sexually transmitted disease. Or like so many, be bound by an "addiction drip" which is delivering death one drop at a time.

It's quite possible that some of us could be so twisted in our minds from the perverseness of our lifestyle that nothing makes sense. Or ultimately we could already be dead and gone from the face of the earth into an eternity without God.

We should also thank the Lord it isn't "revelation shall follow me all the days of my life" or some of us would be "Public Scoundrel Number One" without a friend in the world and not enough gas to out-drive our shame.

Thank God it is *"Goodness and mercy shall follow me"* so that I can leave my yesterdays trustfully with Him. When the Lord shepherds your life, the will of God happens to you. And it is only at the end the "look back" brings the fullness of this wonderful discovery. In the meantime, however, we *"walk by faith and not by sight"* (2 Corinthians 5:7) and *"Therefore we do not lose heart. Though outwardly we are wasting away, yet inwardly we are being renewed day by day. For our light and momentary troubles are achieving for us an eternal glory that far outweighs them all. So we fix our eyes not on what is seen, but on what is unseen. For what is seen is temporary, but what is unseen is eternal"* (2 Corinthians 4:16-18).

———————— ⚡ ————————

Be confident that every one of our prayers
yet unanswered will outlive us.

Long after our voice has been silenced by death, unanswered prayer rises before the Lord from heaven's altar (Revelation 6:9-10). Even in this we can say with David, *"Surely I have a delightful inheritance."*

THE PERSONIFICATION OF "GOOD"

The Holy Spirit gives us two words which characterize the Father's dealing with those whom He is allowed to shepherd their life. They are *"goodness"* and *"mercy." "Goodness"* (towb/Hebrew) means that which is "ethically good and right; contributing positively to the outcome or condition of a situation; pleasant to the higher nature; appropriate, valuable, and best in estimation; having a sense of gladness, favor and prosperity."

This one word *"goodness"* gives us the fullest description of what governs God's motives, reasons, inspiration and desired outcome in all of His dealings with His Children. Good is not just something He does. Good is what He *is*. He can respond to us in no other way because He is the personification of good.

The word *"mercy"* (checed/Hebrew) (eleos/Greek) in the original is "lovingkindness, faithfulness, steadfast love." It also implies "the outward manifestation of pity." Three basic meanings of the word *"mercy"* always interact. They are "strength," "steadfastness," and "love." Any understanding of the word that fails to suggest all three synonyms inevitably loses some of its richness in meaning.

"Love" by itself easily becomes sentimentalized or universalized apart from the commitment of a covenant. Yet "strength" or "steadfastness" suggests only the fulfillment of a legal or other obligation. In its fullness, the word *mercy* contains the idea of living up to a commitment not just by contractual agreement, but because of unwavering love that has made such a commitment. Yet "checed" (mercy) is not only a matter of obligation; it is one of generosity. It is not just an issue of loyalty, but also of pity.

The weaker party seeks the protection and blessing of the one who is the stronger. But the weaker has no absolute claim to it. The stronger party remains committed to his promise, yet retains his freedom and rightful privilege—especially with regard to the manner in which he will fulfill those promises.

"LOVER AND LEADER"

This is the mercy of God toward those whose lives He has given shepherding influence. Marital love is often related to "checed" (mercy). Marriage certainly is a legal matter, and there are legal sanctions for infractions. Yet the relationship, if sound, far transcends mere legalities.

"Checed" implies personal involvement and commitment in a relationship beyond the rule of law.

Paul speaks in these terms of our relationship with the Lord. He describes this using marriage as the image. *"I am jealous for you with a godly jealousy. I promised you to one husband, to Christ, so that I might present you as a pure virgin to Him"* (2 Corinthians 11:2). In the allusion of Christ the husband to His bride the church, Jesus is presented to us as lover and leader, protector and provider—and we are lost in the embrace of His mercy.

MERCY, GOODNESS AND THE HOUSEHOLD OF GOD

When the Lord shepherds my life, my dismal yesterday is transformed into a gloriously hopeful tomorrow. *"And I shall dwell in the house of the Lord forever."*

This statement is not some mindless escapism. Neither does the promise of *"surely goodness and mercy shall follow me"* communicate the idea that because of mercy and goodness, God is going to come along behind me with a huge "pooper-scooper" and clean up my messes. And therefore I can just go through life irresponsibly leaving a mess.

The *"house of the Lord"* is a reference to the heaven I am promised, even if it is further down the road. It also means a life of right relationship with the Lord and with other members of the family of God, here and now.

Every tomorrow begins today. I live today and order my life against the backdrop of forever, and it is always in the context of right relationships with others. Through communion with Christ we are already "dwelling in the house of the Lord."

The word *"house"* (bayith/Hebrew) is translated "household; family dwelling." To *"dwell"* (yashab'/Hebrew) means "to settle, to remain, to inhabit, to marry, to have as ones living place." If I already possess "eternal life" and yet I am waiting for eternity, then I am already dwelling in the *"house of the Lord,"* awaiting the forever *"mansions"* Jesus said are part of the Father's house (John 14:2).

Paul declared our gathering together in fellowship, worship and ministry as the church is that *"house of the Lord"* today. *"But you have come to Mount Zion, to the heavenly Jerusalem, the city of the living God. You have come to thousands upon thousands of angels in joyful assembly, to the church of the firstborn, whose names are written in heaven. You have come to God, the judge of all men, to the spirits of righteous men made perfect, to Jesus the mediator of a new covenant..."* (Hebrews 12:22-24). *"You are no longer strangers and foreigners, but citizens with the saints and members of the household of God"* (Ephesians 2:19 NKJV).

IT SHALL "FOLLOW ME"

When the Lord is my Shepherd, *"goodness and mercy"* are also what follow in the wake of my life lived in relationship to the rest of the family in the household of God. *"Goodness and mercy"* is how I relate to them and they to me. It is characteristic of our alliances in the family. The goodness and mercy of God is evident through me to others, and that's the impact their life is to have upon mine.

In His parable of the Good Samaritan Jesus asks, " *'Which of these three do you think was a neighbor to the man who fell into the hands of robbers?' The expert in the law replied, 'The one who had mercy on him'. Jesus told him, 'Go and do likewise'"* (Luke 10:36-37).

Mercy is more than someone's motivational gift. It is the outflow of what I have been a recipient of. David said *"surely* (ak/Hebrew) *goodness and mercy shall follow me."* This is God saying, "It is emphatically certain that when I shepherd your life you can trust your yesterdays to My *'goodness and mercy.'* And it will be My *'goodness and mercy'* you will touch others with in the wake of your living in my household—a household which is both now and eternally yet to come."

If not *"goodness and mercy"* then what do we have in the house of the Lord but division and criticism? Merciless judgmentalism in the church is such a travesty that only the all-knowing of God's holy, judicial discernment in eternity can and will reveal it.

When we think of how many souls have been lost to the church and to heaven because of this, it should leave us short of breath in a wondering expectancy of *"that day"* when the Chief Shepherd of the flock will bring the hidden things to light. *"Therefore judge nothing before the appointed time; wait till the Lord comes. He will bring to light what is hidden in darkness and will expose the motives of men's hearts. At that time each will receive his praise from God"* (1 Corinthians 4:5).

To think of how the ministry power, effectiveness and Kingdom relevance of many congregations has been assaulted, dishonored and diminished because of this should be a fountainhead of grief to our hearts.

FINDING GOD'S GOODNESS AND MERCY ENCOMPASSES A LIFETIME

The goodness and mercy of God not only deals with the failures of my past, but it secures the blessing and prosperity of my future. If Christ Jesus is shepherding my life, then as my Shepherd those *"paths of righteousness"* which are for *"His name's sake"* are also for my blessing and joy. Since He knows me better than I know myself or am willing to admit, then in all things He will always be better to me than I or anybody else will. But there are times when those *"paths of righteousness"* seem anything but righteous, good or fair. Sometimes those paths involve the unfair treatment by others, and even extremely adverse circumstances which result from the careless and downright sinful actions of others.

Jesus made a powerfully promising declaration which speaks to this issue. *"Let me assure you that no one has ever given up anything—home, brothers, sisters, mother, father, children, or property—for love of Me and to tell others the Good News, who won't be given back, a hundred times over, homes, brothers, sisters, mothers, children, and land-with persecutions! All these will be his here on earth, and in the world to come he shall have eternal life"* (Mark 10:29-30 TLB).

First, Jesus was saying that God won't be a debtor to anyone. His blessing and reward will always be in abundance, *"a hundred times over"* what we may have given up in this world. Our biggest problem with all of this is to accept the fact God's payday isn't always on Friday!

Second, none of this happens except *"with persecutions."* The word *"persecutions"* (dioko/Greek) means "to drive away, put to flight, pursue." The nature of life in Christ's Kingdom is such a struggle because there is an enemy who opposes our Kingdom life and work. There is a spiritual adversary who is a thief coming to steal, kill and destroy at every turn (John 10:10). His work is to "pursue" us in an attempt to "drive us away" from trust and obedience and "put to flight" our confidence in God. Ultimately he undertakes to kill our joy, destroy our life of faith and steal from us the blessing and favor God has promised.

There will be difficulties encountered for which Jesus doesn't explain or make excuses. He just states emphatically that it will be *"with persecutions."*

Third, Jesus was saying that the same goodness and mercy which dealt with our past failures will secure the blessings of our future. The Son of God declares, *"All these will be his here on earth, and in the world to come he shall have eternal life."* David also wrote, *"And I shall dwell in the house of the Lord forever."* It's the same truth, just stated in different terms. It is God's goodness and mercy following after, traveling with, and going before—securing the blessings and prosperity of my future.

In the midst of the journey we just don't know how it is all going to work out. But we know it will, because it involves a lifetime of encountering the goodness and mercy of the Lord, past, present and yet to come.

A NEW COUNTENANCE

Recently, I sat with a dear friend and his wife as they shared their story with me. It serves to illustrate this great truth.

Gene and Arlene have been friends of mine and my wife's for nearly the past 30 years. Gene is a born again believer and a physician who befriended me in my second year of full-time ministry. He became a jogging partner, a trusted friend, encourager and a "father" in the faith.

When he received the forgiveness of Christ he was radically and forever changed. His third marriage was to Arlene, a wonderful Christian lady. And I remember seeing a portrait of him hanging in the hallway of their home taken before he had come to Christ. The difference in countenance and demeanor that reflected the spirit of an unbeliever in that picture, by comparison to the peace and love of Christ he reflects today, was so evident in the portrait that we talked about it.

Gene was passionate concerning his walk with the Lord and deeply burdened for those around him who needed the Savior. Having been the head of the psychosomatic illness department in a hospital in the south, Gene also had a wealth of knowledge concerning health and human behavior.

His counseling expertise and ability in applying the truths of God's Word in practical ways to address psychosomatic related physical symptoms was always a help to those who would take the time to listen. Eventually his counsel became the material of a book he authored entitled, "Divine Healing." Much of his basic concepts became the source of my encouragement and counsel for congregants who requested spiritual and pastoral guidance.

The city where we lived and where he practiced medicine was also his mission field. He spearheaded many citywide outreach crusades hosting a number of guests. Most notably was the Rev. David Wilkerson, who was an evangelist at the time.

Gene's heart for the sick, hurting and lost always came through when he would meet with pastors in the city and tried to convince them of the need to come together for such an outreach. I remember sitting in those meetings thinking that if the pastors of the city had the same compassion for the lost as Dr. Gene, we could actually take the city for Christ in one of those crusades.

I know this was his dream. But as is the case so many times, leadership's differences in philosophy of ministry and evangelism always seemed to undermine the full Kingdom potential for such an event.

HE KNEW THE "GREAT PHYSICIAN"

Dr. Gene's compassion for the sick, hurting and lost was also profoundly demonstrated in his medical practice. His patient list included those on welfare and the indigent who could get medical care nowhere else simply because doctors filled their schedule with paying patients. The revenue loss from such a patient policy was huge. And yet he would tend to their physical needs, at times even providing prescription medications for free.

Today like never before, when "time is money" in the medical industry, Dr. Gene would take extra care to speak with patients about the troubling issues in their life and offer godly counsel from the Word and from his own life experiences. "Doc" would also purchase large quantities of medicine and personally schedule a week away from the practice in order to take the healing and hope which comes from medicine and the Gospel of Christ to third world nations.

On occasion I would accompany him on rounds at the hospital. Before we left each room, Dr. Gene would gently lay his hand upon his patient and pray for Christ's healing and delivering power to be their's. He was a devoted practitioner of applying the healing science of medicine and the healing power of the Word of God.

Many times I myself was the recipient of his gracious counsel as well as skillful medical care. I never forgot him saying to me one day, "Terry, Jesus is the Great Physician. All the rest of us doctors are just interns." But such a spiritual ministry and medical practice is not without opposition. Jesus said it would be *"with persecutions"* and it was just that for Dr. Gene.

A DESTROYED PRACTICE

The Catholic hospital in town was not very receptive to "Doc's" approach. In fact the Catholic nuns openly opposed his prayer with patients and continuously complained to the hospital administration. But he persevered and the Holy Spirit pursued the hearts of people.

Then after thirty years of a spotless medical record in that city, "Doc" performed two procedures— the results of which were not life threatening— to the patient but certainly less than desired in outcome. It was the opportunity his opposition in the medical and administrative staff manipulated to pressure a review.

The examination he submitted to came back hostile to him personally and the chance to scandalize his reputation and ruin his practice was eagerly seized upon. In a matter of weeks he became a high risk for his insurance carrier and the cost of his policies skyrocketed. By the time he considered legal action to protect himself, the losses were so great that together with legal costs to fight the "persecution," it simply would not be feasible. This incident, combined with the fact he refused to bow to the pressures of joining an HMO which had come into town, brought a thirty year practice to an end in less than one year.

Bankruptcy ensued, properties were sold and his practice was given over to his partner who had joined the HMO. Instead of retirement at the end of a life-long medical practice, there was hardly a chance to start over doing anything.

At a time like this try quoting *"surely goodness and mercy shall follow me all the days of my life"* with any sense of a glowing testimony and a straight look on your face! But in fact, that's exactly the dynamic which was at work. It started with the salvation of a doctor at the hospital who had observed the entire proceedings which had culminated in Dr. Gene's demise. This doctor had also been witness to "Doc's" personal life and testimony as a follower of Jesus Christ.

This physician told Dr. Gene he had observed an obvious conspiracy against him. So he wrote a letter of recommendation to vindicate "Doc." And then he said, "Even though I was raised a Catholic, I want you to know that seeing Christ in you has convinced me of the reality of needing to find Him as my own personal Savior. My wife and I and our family have given our lives to Jesus because of the witness of your life."

Those days of loss, desperation and great personal need were really the prelude to God's "Friday" for Dr. Gene and Arlene.

Without them really knowing it at first, *"goodness and mercy"* had followed them the whole way and now it was God's "payday." What had been given up because of insurmountable opposition for the love of Christ and in order to share with others this Gospel was about to be multiplied back in the *"hundred fold"* Jesus promised.

A Multiplied Ministry

When Rev. David Wilkerson, now the founder and pastor of Time Square Church with its multiplied outreach to the inner city of New York heard of their situation he appointed them medical missionaries of Time Square Church. What had begun twenty years earlier as a ministry relationship to reach a city was about to become a ministry partnership of reaching nations. God's mercy and goodness was following and securing the Lord's blessing and provision for the future.

Today "Doc" and Arlene are doing what has been the passion of their hearts all along. They are treating the sick and freely preaching the Gospel of Christ to the poor, the hurting and the lost. They have even gone into prisons of Latin American countries where the most dangerous gang members with ties to New York City are incarcerated. There they found a receptivity which had not been given to others. They are a manifestation of the healing and delivering love and power of Christ to the hopeless and hurting in a miraculous way.

The free prescription medications Doc used to give to those who couldn't afford them are being multiplied back hundreds-fold through the ministry of Time Square Church. The one-week medical missions trips he used to take away from his practice and put on his own credit card are being multiplied back six to eight months out of every year and all expenses paid. And the tenuous income from a sacrificially-giving medical practice has been replaced by a medical missions salary and a residence in the San Francisco Bay area. Not to mention the freedom and joy of doing what he always prayed and dreamed of doing but couldn't until the "persecution" removed the obstacles.

Today, Doc can look at you with a straight face, a confident testimony and say, *"Surely goodness and mercy shall follow me all the days of my life"* and make a believer out of you! And not only you and me, but the thousands on his "hundred-fold" patient list which includes several third world countries.

What mercy! What goodness!

PART III

~~~—— ·*MM·* ——~~~

WHEN THE LORD
SHEPHERDS
HIS CHURCH

Among the many expressions of praise and calls to worship, David penned one in terms of the Good Shepherd and His sheep. *"Oh come, let us worship and bow down; Let us kneel before the LORD our Maker. For He is our God. And we are the people of His pasture, and the sheep of His hand"* (Psalm 95:6-7 NKJV).

The prophet Micah was given the same prophetic picture with reference to national Israel's relationship to Jesus the Messiah during His millennial rule on earth. *"He will stand and shepherd His flock in the strength of the LORD, in the majesty of the name of the LORD His God. And they will live securely, for then His greatness will reach to the ends of the earth"* (Micah 5:4). And the writer of the Book of Hebrews speaks in terms of the Lord Jesus' shepherding influence actively equipping and empowering His church to accomplish His work in the world. *"May the God of peace, who through the blood of the eternal covenant brought back from the dead our Lord Jesus, that great Shepherd of the sheep, equip you with everything good for doing His will, and may He work in us what is pleasing to Him, through Jesus Christ, to whom be glory for ever and ever. Amen"* (Hebrews 13:20-21).

In his first letter to the early church, the apostle Peter admonished the leadership to, *"Be shepherds of God's flock that is under your care, serving as overseers—not because you must, but because you*

169

are willing, as God wants you to be; not greedy for money, but eager to serve; not lording it over those entrusted to you, but being examples to the flock. And when the Chief Shepherd appears, you will receive the crown of glory that will never fade away" (1 Peter 5:1-4). His exhortation to these under-shepherds was in the context of their accountability to the Chief Shepherd, the Lord Jesus Christ, who would reward them for their servant leadership under His shepherding oversight.

"I KNOW YOUR DEEDS"

In the opening chapters of the Book of Revelation we are given the vision of Jesus standing in the midst of His church in Asia. These seven churches did not comprise a denomination and their only affiliation was to Jesus. So the living message today is to *any* church which lays claims to the name of Jesus Christ regardless of denominational affiliation.

One remarkable revelation is of Jesus standing outside of His church in Laodicea asking to be given entrance. The picture given to us is one of Christ's church conducting its business and administrating its program, seemingly oblivious to the fact that the true Pastor had no influence or authority.

Jesus' message to these believers was, *"I know your deeds, that you are neither cold nor hot. I wish you were either one or the other! So, because you are lukewarm— neither hot nor cold—I am about to spit you out of My mouth. You say, 'I am rich; I have acquired wealth and do not need a thing.' But you do not realize that you are wretched, pitiful, poor, blind and naked. I counsel you to buy from Me gold refined in the fire, so you can become rich; and white clothes to wear, so you can cover your shameful nakedness; and salve to put on your eyes, so you can see. Those whom I love I rebuke and discipline. So be earnest, and repent. Here I am! I stand at the door and knock. If anyone hears My voice and opens the door, I will come in and eat with him, and he with Me"* (Revelation 3:15-20).

I contend there is a church that belongs to Jesus in name only. It is one where He personally has little or no influence. It is not defined by a religious denomination, nor by a *lack* of affiliation—since there is no connection with the Lord.

The true church is found in individual, local congregations and includes those who gather in store fronts, school halls and theaters to those who assemble in posh facilities on multi-acreage campuses. The issue is Jesus seeks entrance so He might carry on through them the work and ministry He delegated to His church by the Holy Spirit as recorded for us in the Book of Acts.

The Lord seeks an open-door invitation so He might come and pastor His church.

A SHOCKING STUDY

George Barna posted on his website the following information in his annual review of significant religious findings in the U.S. for the year 2004. The information was gathered through telephone surveys conducted in the nation throughout the year by the Barna Group. The research method and sampling used projected a 95% confidence level. I offer the following statistical information to lend some credibility to the belief that the scenario John received regarding the Laodicean church is as much a present day reality as it was then. Barna titled these findings as "Disappointing Realities."

- The number of unchurched adults in the U.S. has doubled since 1991.
- Born again Christians' connection to Christ makes no difference in the rate of divorce when compared to non-born again adults. Born again Christians divorce their mates at the same rate as unbelievers.
- Christian faith has a limited effect on people's behavior, whether related to moral convictions and practices, relational activities, lifestyle choices or economic practices. Only less than 10% of all evangelical Christians were the exception to this. These make up only 7% of the total population.
- Just half of all Protestant senior pastors (51%) meet the criteria for personally having a biblical world view. The

criteria for having such a view are:

1. Believing God is the all-knowing and all-powerful creator of the universe who still rules today.
2. That Jesus Christ never sinned.
3. That Satan is real.
4. That salvation is received through a faith in Christ, not by good deeds.
5. That every follower of Christ has a responsibility to share their faith with non-believers.
6. That the Bible is accurate in all it teaches.
7. That absolute moral truth exists.
8. That absolute moral truth is described in the Bible.

- Tithing is pitifully uncommon. And it is almost non-existent among people under the age of 40. Only 7% of born again Christian adults tithed last year.
- Born again Christians and adults who attend Christian churches are more likely than atheists, agnostics, and adherents of non-Christian faiths to buy lottery tickets.
- Female pastors are substantially different in their theological beliefs than are male pastors. They tend to be much more liberal in their views, are less likely to have a biblical world view, are less likely to be born-again, and more likely to have been divorced.
- There seems to be a consistent degree of attrition of men from the Christian faith. The numbers of men who are un-churched is rising, while the numbers of men who are "deeply spiritual" and those who possess an active faith (attend church, pray and read the Bible during the week) is declining.
- Half of all Christian adults are so satisfied with their spiritual life that there is nothing at all they wish to change or improve in the future.

Most Americans do not accept the notion they are engaged in a spiritual battle. This is fueled by widespread rejection of the notion Satan is real, salvation is by faith alone, and by the common acceptance of the idea that there are multiple paths to salvation. This also partially explains why only half of all self-described "Christians" are not "absolutely committed" to the Christian faith.

A NEW REVELATION IS NEEDED

All of the above "Disappointing Realities" are a contradiction to the promises and teachings of Jesus Himself and the apostles concerning the power of the Gospel and the ministry of Christ's church. They stand in stark contrast to Jesus' characterization of the church He said He would be building here on earth until He returned. For He told us it would be a church the restraining, diminishing and life-quenching boundaries of hell's gates could not prevail against (Matthew16:18).

He said it would be one where greater works than He had done, not in kind but in number, would be performed (John 14:12). Furthermore, there would be continuing signs of healing, spiritual gifts and power over demonic entities demonstrated by this church as they declared His Gospel (Matthew 16:17-18).

Jesus also said it would be a church which gave itself to the task of world evangelism and it would take the message of the Gospel to every people group, and then He would return (Matthew 24:14).

Could it be that the Holy Spirit's greatest task today is not in bringing conviction unto salvation to this lost world, but rather first to bring repentance unto conversion to the church? What if the Lord visited our sinful cities exerting great conviction by the presence of His Holy Spirit? Which churches would it be safe for Him to send seekers who in response to such conviction came broken in heart and contrite in spirit?

What would be the invitation of the church to these seekers? Would it be, "Come and join us and become like us"? Or would it be, "Come and join us and become like Jesus"?

There is needed today, as in every generation, a revelation of the resurrected Christ—Jesus personally and powerfully present, pastoring His church and shepherding His people.

173

John received what he called the "Revelation of Jesus Christ." Though it included a divine view of the end times, of the church in the last days, and of the Antichrist, it was not first and foremost an unveiling of these things. It is the revelation of Jesus Christ.

A HEAVENLY INSIGHT

John's revelation was not a spiritual life report, or a position paper formulated as the result of religious research, scholarly consideration and majority consensus. What he saw was neither a dream, a fantasy, or the imagination of a religious fanatic spending too much time alone under the duress of incarceration. This heavenly insight came by a direct angelic visitation (Revelation 1:1) and when John was in prayer, *"in the Spirit on the Lord's day"* (v.9). It came by a personal encounter with the risen Jesus, The Good Shepherd, and Chief Shepherd of the flock.

The Book of Revelation is not to be read first and foremost as a look at future events. When this is the church's focus we spend our time searching for signs and debating the events of the last days, particularly when the church is going to "get raptured." When the Book of Revelation is read as a presentation of the person of Jesus to His church, then the focus becomes one of *"looking unto Jesus the Author and Finisher of our faith"* (Hebrews.12:2 NKJV).

―――――――――

A church which seeks such a revelation of Jesus will encounter Him powerfully present in her midst. You cannot be "in the Spirit on the Lord's day" and not have a revelation of Jesus in the church.

Generally speaking, there is a sense in the body of Christ today that Jesus is in heaven interceding and waiting for the appointed time when He will return to "kick satanic posterior" and fix the problems of this world through His personal reign. But in the meantime we must just go on with our church business and religious work as best as we know how until that time comes. But the Book of Revelation is the

174

disclosure of His presence in the church here and now!

Jesus says, *"I am with you always even to the end of the age"* (Matthew 28:20 NKJV). *"Where two or three come together in My name, there I am with them"* (Matthew18:20). *"And I will ask the Father, and He will give you another Counselor to be with you forever the Spirit of truth. The world cannot accept Him, because it neither sees Him nor knows Him. But you know Him, for He lives with you and will be in you. I will not leave you as orphans; I will come to you"* (John 14:16-18).

He was promising to be personally present among His people, presiding over the life and ministry of His church. The opening chapters of the Book of Revelation are the declaration of the literal fulfillment of this fact. He is the One who is in the *"midst of the seven lampstands"* which are His churches (Revelation 1:13).

It is the scene of Jesus present with His people in communion and fellowship. He is sovereignly superintending and overseeing the life and ministry of His church. He is walking in their midst, never idle but always working by His Holy Spirit caring for and providing for His followers. He is the One opening doors for His church that no man can close; open doors He calls upon His people to walk through by faith and obedience.

A RECEPTIVE HEART

Contrast this picture with the one George Barna's statistics portray of the church in America. Jesus has admonitions for each congregation that are uniquely their's. He knows each intimately, yet He gives one exhortation which is the same to all seven churches. *"He who has an ear to hear, let him hear what the Spirit says to the churches."*

A "hearing ear" is the image of a receptive heart. Hearing requires integrity of heart to accept the Word of the Lord as absolute truth. It involves a soul desire to honestly hear the Word; to receive it without prejudice or pre-dispositional bias.

The "Spirit speaking" is the Voice behind the voice and the printed page. It is heard in the heart and the Holy Spirit presses its truth, authority, revelation, illumination, comfort and instruction powerfully upon our spirit. You can feel it when it happens. It's more than a light of understanding clicking on upstairs; it is a fire of personal revelation igniting and burning within.

The Word of God was not given to make us smart, it was delivered to change our lives. This requires more than truth. Jesus said, *"You will know the truth and the truth will set you free"* (John 8:32).

It isn't just the truth which liberates us, it is *knowing* the truth. This knowledge requires the Holy Spirit speaking. It is *"to the churches"* Christ is directing His words.

Each congregation has its functional and/or dysfunctional characteristics of fellowship and ministry by virtue of the personal lives of the individuals who comprise the body of believers.

Every church has a individual life and ministry dynamic distinctly its own. It is unique by virtue of the vision and mission God has given to its pastoral leadership and embraced by its membership in unity and faith. To the degree this is happening in a local church, such a body realizes its God-given destiny in its city.

This alone explains much concerning the success or failure of local congregations. Every church has its mortality; its duration of usefulness to the Kingdom of God in the earth which is distinctly its own.

THE NEXT LEVEL

I heard Bill Hybels, pastor of Willow Creek Church in Illinois, state this truth powerfully in a leadership meeting held at Bayside Church of Granite Bay, California. He was offering his commendations to this truly great congregation for their vision and willingness to give themselves to the mission on their tenth year anniversary.

Hybles stated there is always a reason the favor of God falls upon a church. It suggests a journey which is dynamic and it portends a future in God that is one of greater things. This is evidence of the sovereign and divine dimension which transcends the human. But the temptation is to settle down and enjoy the favor and blessing rather than step up to the next level of faith and works.

There are no "Kodak moments" in the work of God. A church will either become better or worse, healthier or sicker, more or less dynamic for God.

Hybles told of how Willow Creek Church was faced with decision-making times either to step it up in faith, or settle back into something from which they may never recover. For the church that is always willing to move higher, God is willing to prove Himself a thousand times in the process of fulfilling the dream He has given.

The Book of Revelation is first the picture of Jesus pastoring His church and shepherding His flock with the promise of taking them through to the end of the age—if they are willing to have an ear which hears what the Spirit is saying. This final book of the Bible shows how prophetic end time events are tended to and influenced by unseen spiritual forces at work. There are the warring of angelic hosts against the powers of demonic entities. There is the sovereign appointing and setting aside of leaders of nations by the hand of God to bring them into line with the fulfillment of His purpose and plan.

In addition, there is the intercessory praying and the preaching of the Gospel by the church in witness to the world with accompanying signs and wonders of salvation, healings, deliverance and miracles by the Holy Spirit. There is also the fulfillment of His promise to national Israel. But the focus of Christ's personal attention and desire is to make Himself known, to be powerfully present in His church. And that presence is identified as the "Spirit of Christ" (Romans 8:9; 1 Peter 1:11).

REVELATION, REALIZATION AND RELEASE

If Christ is the Chief Shepherd of the flock, then there are evidences of His shepherding influence which are unmistakable. The Book of Revelation reveals a vivid view of Jesus who has come to pastor His church. It is an insight the Lord wants us to know by experience so we can become what His church is to be in the outworking and fulfillment of end time events.

When Jesus shepherds His church there is the evidence of His person, His power, and His presence.

In these closing chapters let us consider more fully these evidences:

1. There is a revelation of the person of Jesus which brings life transformation.
2. There is a realization of the presence of Jesus that is the true stimulus for worship.
3. There is a release of the resurrection power of Jesus to advance the Kingdom of Christ.

CHAPTER ELEVEN

A REVELATION OF THE PERSON OF JESUS THAT BRINGS LIFE TRANSFORMATION

"I saw...someone 'like a son of man', dressed in a robe reaching down to his feet and with a golden sash around His chest. His head and hair were white like wool, as white as snow, and His eyes were like blazing fire. His feet were like bronze glowing in a furnace, and His voice was like the sound of rushing waters. In His right hand He held seven stars, and out of His mouth came a sharp double-edged sword. His face was like the sun shining in all its brilliance."

– REVELATION 1:12-16

On the island of Patmos, John encountered Jesus as he had never seen Him before. In his Gospel he writes, *"And the Word became flesh and dwelt among us, and we beheld His glory, the glory as of the only begotten of the Father, full of grace and truth"* (John 1:14 NKJV).

This is what John saw as He walked with Jesus during the days of His earthly ministry. The teaching of Christ had brought to the world the fullness of the truth of the Father. His miracle ministry and atoning death was the demonstration of the grace of God. Everything about His life, ministry and atoning death was a fulfillment of prophecy. Jesus embodied the glory of God's grace and truth.

IT IS THE ASCENDED AND GLORIFIED JESUS WHO INHABITS HIS CHURCH

However, John encountered a glorified Jesus which brought him to the ground, as faint as a dead man. No longer was the Lord just the itinerant teacher and miracle worker, a lover and blesser of children, a forgiver of prostitutes and crooked politicians, a chastiser of hypocritical religious leaders, a healer, a suffering servant, a bleeding and dying prophet or even a resurrected Savior.

Now John is in the presence of Jesus the glorified Son of God. He is the *"First and the Last,"* the eternal One. The One whose final prayer John recorded in his gospel is in part now being fulfilled. *"Father, I want those You have given Me to be with Me where I am, and to see My glory, the glory You have given Me because You loved me before the creation of the world"* (John 17:24).

John saw it was the glorified Jesus who inhabits heaven.

The seamless robe the woman with the issue of blood reached out in faith and touched for her healing; the simple garment which was stripped from Him by the soldiers of execution and gambled away at the foot of His cross; those grave clothes which wrapped His bruised and torn body and the cloth that covered His face, have been replaced by a glistening robe of celestial royalty and a shining breastplate of gold.

His head which had few places on earth to lay in rest, and His hair which had been reduced to a bloody, tangled mess ensnarled in thorns, has become the dazzling white display of infinite wisdom and seniority that shines as bright as the sun.

His eyes which wept at Lazarus' tomb, and over Jerusalem's impending judgment; eyes bloodshot in Gethsemane's agonizing prayer vigil; eyes that faded to death's empty stare upon the Cross, are now as a flame of fire which pierce the soul in all-knowing conviction.

One fiery glance from those eyes on judgment day and the eternal value of every Christian's life's work will either go up in smoke as hay, wood and grass or be purged to the purest of gold, silver and precious stones.

His voice which summoned the dead, dispossessed demons from their human hosts, commanded healing to the sick and infirm, pronounced deliverance to the slaves of darkness, declared truth to the victims of falsehood, spoke forgiveness to the sinful and eternal hope to failures in life, is now the trumpeting voice of final judgment and consummate authority which snaps every nerve in John's body to attention.

But John also saw it is this same glorified Jesus who also walks among the seven lampstands. He is all that He was when His physical presence graced Palestine. But He is more—for He is the One who *"is and who was and who is to come, the Almighty"* (Revelation.1:8).

The point is: it is the glorified Jesus who comes to possess His church.

IT IS ALL ABOUT THE LORD

The only glory there is for the church is the one a revelation of the person of Jesus brings. This is not found in the church's financial and real estate holdings, creative ministry programs, social and political influence or trained and gifted leadership. While these are all wonderful ministry assets which can be utilized in communicating a contemporary biblical message, it is in a revelation of the person of Jesus that is transpiring in the church which becomes the church's glory.

Paul writes, *"To Him be the glory in the church and in Christ Jesus to all generations forever and ever. Amen"* (Ephesians 3:21). When Jesus is given center stage He will accept it. He declares, *"But I, when I am lifted up from the earth, will draw all men to Myself"* (John 12:32).

There must be a strategy for ministry—and this blueprint is the mission that flows from a God-given vision to the pastoral leadership for a local congregation. However, we can emphasize a ministry philosophy, style or doctrinal distinctive to the point where those become the identifying characteristics we think is the most important image to project in giving the American "church shopping" customer an attractive choice.

The yellow pages of any local phone directory is one of the best ways to see how churches identify themselves. You'll find advertisements which emphasize Word of Faith, Deeper Life, Holiness, Missionary, Traditional, Contemporary, Denominational, Charismatic, Community, Family, Pentecostal, Nondenominational, Seeker Friendly, Prophetic, Tabernacle of David Worship, Apostolic, Full Gospel and more. You can even find what appears at first glance to be a "Coffee Café Church"—because that fellowship feature is prominent in the advertisement.

I sat one Sunday and listened to the announcements being given in one successful church and the newest smoothie flavor at their espresso bar that day was the highlight! I also heard of one youth group in a large, affluent congregation promoting its oxygen bar.

None of these in themselves are wrong—neither should any church be criticized for offering them. If this is the "hook" which brings people through the door, so be it! However:

- It's going to take more than a cup of flavored coffee to bring life transformation.
- It's going to take more than just practical teaching on principles and disciplines for successful Christian living.
- It's going to take more than Christian concerts, contemporary or otherwise.
- It will take more than accountability to a small group.

These are all needful ministries, but they are not enough if there is no revelation of the person of Jesus to the souls of people by the ministry of the Holy Spirit. This is a "supernatural thing," not a "ministry program" thing.

———————

Life transformation comes when we get a glimpse of the glory of the person of Jesus and realize it's all about Him.

Jesus can't be simply a figure in the background whose name is mentioned from time to time in Bible studies, sermons or conversations as the One who has provided all of what we enjoy. It's not even all about experiencing God's goodness and blessing if I live right. Because I am not saved only to enjoy the Christian life or to just get busy and do church work and make the program a success.

I am saved to become like Him—and only in this way can I glorify and legitimately introduce Him to others. Such a life transformation requires a revelation of the person of Jesus in the ministry and life of the church. He is why I attend the House of God, live a godly life and make the most of my days. He is why I am a faithful employee and an honest employer, why I stay married, why I discipline my children and train them in the way they should live. It is not just so I can enjoy the best life a Christian could ever have.

We are called to be followers of no one else but Jesus Christ—and no one but God's Spirit can make us to be like Him. Jesus said the One who would bring such a revelation of His person to the human soul was the Holy Spirit. *"But when the Helper comes, whom I shall send to you from the Father, the Spirit of truth who proceeds from the Father, He will testify of Me"* (John 15:26 NKJV).

Again, it's really all about Him! *"For in Him we live and, move and have our being"* (Acts 17:28 NKJV). *"For those God foreknew He also predestined to be conformed to the likeness of His Son, that He might be the firstborn among many brothers"* (Romans 8:29). *"...as the Spirit of the Lord works within us, we become more and more like Him"* (2 Corinthians 3:17-18 TLB).

Unless Jesus is given center stage in our living, teaching, preaching, serving, giving and motivation, then regardless of all the good we do, we still can't produce life transformation.

WE CAN TEACH CHRISTIAN MORAL ETHICS AND NOT PREACH CHRIST

The church of Acts placed the person of Jesus at center stage. When Peter spoke on the Day of Pentecost he preached Jesus (Acts 2:14-41). And the Holy Spirit made Christ so real to the hearts of those who listened that three thousand received Christ as their personal Savior.

The resurrection of Jesus is what was proclaimed. His life is what they role modeled; His teaching and the revelational truths the apostles received from the Spirit of Christ is what they preached and taught. The life and ministry of Jesus was the identifying characteristic of the early church.

———— ✐ ————

We can teach the Bible as God's practical laws for right living holding out to us the promises of God's blessing and hope for eternal life. And that they are without a doubt! But we can teach Christian ethics as a moral philosophy and discipline for living and not preach Jesus.

When we declare Christ, we also must present His claims upon our life and His call to full surrender in discipleship. And we have to preach Him for who He is "right now" in the church—because that's how John saw Him among the golden lamp stands. In the church today He is Savior, Lord, Miracle Worker, Divine Healer, Deliverer, Holy Spirit Baptizer, Lord of the Harvest, Captain of the Angelic Host of Heaven, Returning King of kings, and Judge of the Whole Earth. And that's just for starters!

WHAT A REVELATION OF THE PERSON OF JESUS WILL DO FOR US

Acts chapter three is the account of the miracle healing of the lame man at the temple gate. It happened because Peter and John presented the person of Jesus in His fullness to meet the need. It illustrates four things such a revelation will do for us.

1. A revelation of the person of Jesus will arrest our attention, change our perspective and transform our desires.

The lame man was in the best spot to beg. People coming to

worship would be more likely to be compassionate and give him money. He was so focused on asking for alms that when Peter and John came by they had to interrupt his begging and distract him by saying, *"Look at us!"* (Acts 3:4). In other words, get your eyes off the magnitude of your problem and what you perceive to be the answer to your situation and get ready to encounter Jesus.

Even then, the beggar still looked to them thinking they were going to give him money. Peter and John did not call his attention to themselves, rather *away* from what he was looking to as his answer. *"Then Peter said, 'Silver and gold I do not have. But what I do have I give you. In the name of Jesus Christ of Nazareth rise up and walk.' And he took him by the right hand and lifted him up, and immediately his ankle bones received strength. So he, leaping up, stood and walked and entered the temple with them—walking, leaping, and praising God"* (vv.6-8 NKJV).

By the power of the Holy Spirit, the beggar received a revelation of the person of Jesus as the Healer. The now-healed man was no longer outside the gate asking for money. The former cripple didn't even run home and let his family and friends see the miracle which had happened to him. He was in the temple wanting to be near to the place where there was a revelation of the person of Jesus through the ministry of Peter and John.

I would call that a change of perspective and transformation of desire.

2. A revelation of the person of Jesus will give us what we need, not necessarily what we want.

The lame man had two problems. He was crippled and he was poor. What he wanted was a more comfortable and profitable place to beg. But that's not what he *needed.* What he wanted was not in agreement with a revelation of the person of Jesus in his life as Healer.

Sometimes it is the same for us in our Christian experience.

- We want to feel good, but we may need to feel convicted of sin.
- We want entertainment, but we need to worship God.

185

- We want respectability, yet we may need humility.
- We want success and blessing, but we may need repentance and faith.
- We want to hear our favorite music in church, instead we need to hear the voice of the Holy Spirit and the song of the Lord.
- We want church membership and association, but we need to be a witness to our city.
- We want to attend interesting Bible studies, yet we need to obey the command of the Lord.
- We want to sit under good preaching, however, we need to practice righteous living.
- We want to cut back on the church budget and find ways not to have to fund such a huge vision, but we may need to pay our tithes and give sacrificially.
- We want things predictable, when we may need the *"new wine"* of the Holy Spirit to burst some old wineskins.
- We want to justify enjoyable sin, when we need deliverance from bondage.
- We want the church sanctuary to be filled and all the bills paid, when what we need is the glory of God's presence to fill the house and for the saints to have fasted and prayed and filled the prayer room.

3. A revelation of the person of Jesus uncovers the real problems and identifies the real solutions.

This revelation of Jesus as the Healer gave Peter the opportunity to respond to the crowd's inquiry concerning what was happening and point out what the real problems and solutions in the church were. Peter said the issue they faced was because they had *"denied the Holy One"* and *"killed the Prince of Life"* (v.14).

The question involved was what had they done with Jesus? They cut themselves off from His blessing and provision in denying the person of Jesus even though they continued to attend church regularly. It was an issue of the Lord taking His rightful place among them, worthy of all honor, glory and rightful rule.

The solution was: *"...repent and be converted that your sins may be blotted out so that the times of refreshing may come from the Lord, and that He may send Jesus Christ who was preached to you before"* (vv.19-20 NKJV). The real answer was for penitent hearts to turn toward Christ that He might visit them with a refreshing demonstration of who He is.

4. A revelation of the person of Jesus always brings honor to the Scriptures and exalts the Word of God.

Peter was given the open door and proceeded to preach Jesus from the Scriptures as "The Holy One," "Just," "Prince of Life," "Healer," and "Savior" (vv.13-21). He proclaimed Jesus as having fulfilled prophecy, ascended into heaven, and who was coming again.

The written Word came alive because they had received a revelation of the person of Jesus, the Living Word.

The salvation experience of a young Jewish man several years ago illustrates how a revelation of the person of Jesus is what brings life transformation.

EPHRAIM'S ENCOUNTER

When I was a youth pastor in the state of Washington, I joined a friend and together we traveled to San Francisco to participate in an inner city outreach to the "Tenderloin District" hosted by evangelist David Wilkerson. As I remember it then, this area was notoriously a home to bars, adult book and video stores and beats for prostitutes. A small store front had been rented and a coffee house had been opened as a center for ministry operations.

The entire team—who had gathered from across the country—was assigned in shifts either to street ministry or to work the coffee house to minister to those who would drop in.

One evening my friend and I were near the wharf handing out David Wilkerson's latest book entitled, "Two of Me." We were engaging people in conversation and inviting them to the coffee house. One young man walked by, then turned and came back to talk. He stopped because he recognized the name David Wilkerson. We found out he was Ephraim and that he was familiar with Wilkerson's ministry in New York. He had lived there and had even gone to church a little but had rejected Christianity as the answer for himself and had migrated to San Francisco.

He said he was playing in a band and they had a "gig" in one of the bars. I told him I enjoyed the keyboard and would be playing some at the coffee house and invited him to stop by. The next evening we were at the coffee house when Ephraim showed up. We talked music for awhile and when he mentioned he also sang, I asked him to sing something and I would accompany him.

He replied, "I don't sing church songs." When I asked if he knew "Amazing Grace," he smiled and agreed to try it. He began to sing and did reasonably well until he got to the point where the lyrics say, "I once was lost, but now I'm found..."

At that point he abruptly stopped singing. When I looked at him, his face was buried in his hands and he was shaking so badly he had to sit down. Crumpled into the chair, he began to sob openly and blurt out a prayer of repentance and confession like I had never heard before.

Ephriam was openly thanking God for his praying grandmother who had never given up on him. And he was asking the Lord for forgiveness.

In an instant, the Holy Spirit had taken the simple words of a song which spoke of personal salvation and brought to this young man a revelation of the person of Jesus. He realized Christ was the answer to his need for life transformation.

Ephraim checked out of his residence in San Francisco and joined the ministry team in a college dormitory where we were staying. He spent the rest of the week with us on the streets in ministry and then he went through a rehab and discipleship training center associated with World Challenge Ministries.

The last I heard, he was living for Christ and involved in an outreach ministry in Texas. This young Jewish man received Jesus as

His personal Messiah in those moments when the Holy Spirit sovereignly brought the very same revelation of the person of Jesus that John received. *"To Him who loves us and has freed us from our sins by His blood, and has made us to be a kingdom and priests to serve His God and Father—to Him be glory and power for ever and ever! Amen"* (Revelation 1:5-6).

When the Lord shepherds His church there will be a divine revelation of the person of Jesus by the ministry of the Holy Spirit which brings dynamic life transformation.

CHAPTER TWELVE

A REALIZATION OF THE PRESENCE OF JESUS: THE STIMULUS FOR TRUE WORSHIP

"...and among the lampstands was someone like a son of man... When I saw Him, I fell at His feet as though dead."
– REVELATION 1:13, 17

John saw the glorified Christ standing in the midst of the golden lampstands which represented the church.

It is the Lord's rightful place since it is the passionate desire of His heart to be present with His bride when she gathers to "love on" Him in worship and praise.

Let me emphasize that Jesus' call to the lukewarm church of Laodicea, standing outside the door knocking and seeking entrance, is the picture of the reality of a church going on with its religious business and program without the presence of Jesus in her midst. In actuality it doesn't matter what kind of music program a church is privileged to produce, no true worship of Jesus exists in such a place.

CREATING AN ATMOSPHERE FRIENDLY TO THE PRESENCE OF THE LORD

If we are to experience the reality of the Lord shepherding His church we must create an atmosphere which is friendly to His presence. No man ever experienced a time when the presence of God seemed so far removed than Job. And yet Job's statement, *"Though He slay me yet will I hope in Him"* (Job 13:15) is one of the greatest expressions of praise and worship ever uttered.

This created an atmosphere which invited the Lord to be near and it turned Job's suffering into blessing and his mourning into rejoicing.

One of Job's friends, Eliphaz, is the example of saying the right thing at the wrong time. He self-righteously made an accusation against Job during his time of suffering, insinuating Job was being judged for secret sin in his life. And were it not for Job's intercessory ministry in his behalf, Eliphaz would have personally experienced the threat of God's judgment to be a real one.

Nevertheless, Eliphaz made a truthful statement and the Holy Spirit has recorded it for us. *"Now acquaint yourself with Him (God) and be at peace. Thereby good will come to you"* (Job 22:21 NKJV). In other words, when the Lord is your friend, He brings peace and blessing.

One of the stories of Job is that "spiritual atmospheres" surround us daily. The events which transpired in Job's life were directly tied to the activity of his spiritual environment. This was still true even though the significance of the spiritual activity seems mostly unrecognized by Job at the time. He is left to deal with his past in light of His knowledge of God—and of his personal response to Him.

It is precisely in Job's answer to the Lord that he created an atmosphere in the midst of his suffering which was friendly to the presence of God. As a result, the Almighty moved mightily to restore Job and reward him. And that is what worship and praise does. It creates a welcoming atmosphere for the presence of God.

———— ⚜ ————

Spiritual atmospheres are real. We pass through spiritual climates constantly and we live under their influence all the time.

We understand the impact of atmosphere in so many of our choices. Ambience has influence from our choice of restaurants and the detailed preparations for special planned public events or private occasions, to a vacation spot or hotel accommodations.

We've all been in environments where we sense hostility, fear, anxiety, temptation to sin, heaviness and depression, death, intimidation, criticism and other forms of discomfort and uneasiness to our mind and spirit. Our impulse is to want to escape. On the contrary we desire to linger in an atmosphere of joy, comfort, welcome, encouragement, love, friendliness, emotional and spiritual warmth.

"GOOD AND PROFITABLE"

Spiritual environments can't be seen with the human eye or understood by natural senses. God gives us this ability through the *"gift of discerning of spirits"* (1 Corinthians 12:10). This is not the "gift" of a fault-finding attitude or a critical spirit. It is the Holy Spirit's insight for aiding our understanding of the spiritual realm. By it we can gain knowledge of the activity of angelic or demonic spirits in any given circumstance or event—and also perceive the work and ministry of the Holy Spirit in any particular situation. Additionally, we can receive insight into a person's human spirit and motivation.

This enabling by the Holy Spirit is *"...given to each one for the profit of all"* (1 Corinthians 12:7 NKJV). Through this we are equipped to act intelligently, properly, biblically and with godly wisdom in order to minister in the will of God so that good and profit comes to all involved.

Not only are we prepared to react to spiritual atmospheres we encounter, we are to respond proactively in order to create an environment friendly to the presence of God. The counsel of Job's friend Eliphaz, to *"acquaint yourself with God, and be at peace; thereby good will come to you"* is the encouragement to create an atmosphere friendly to the presence of the Lord with the promise of the blessing and provision that God's presence will bring into our lives and circumstances.

193

We cannot expect the peace and blessing of our Heavenly Father if we choose to tolerate a spiritual climate which is not God-friendly. In order for Jesus to shepherd His church, a congregation must choose to create a spiritual atmosphere which welcomes His presence.

ACQUAINTING OURSELVES WITH GOD

The word *"acquaint"* (cakan) has a four-fold application in the Hebrew. Each gives us a fuller understanding of what is meant by creating an atmosphere in my lifestyle and conduct—and one friendly to the presence of God.

1. To acquaint yourself with God means to become familiar with Him.

Moses and Abraham were men who produced an environent which was warm and congenial to the presence of God. When the Lord spoke to Abraham at age 75 to leave his homeland and move his family to Canaan, he did (Genesis 12:1-4).

Abraham fervently believed the Almighty and was called the "friend of God"—and he truly worshiped the Lord. His life is characterized by living in a tent, the picture of obedient faith and building altars of worship.

When God spoke to Moses in the wilderness, he didn't run from the phenomenon of the burning bush. Instead, he stayed and listened and obediently returned to Egypt where he was a wanted man for murder (Exodus 3-4).

His life is defined by obedient faith, which resulted in the demonstration of God's miraculous power. Abraham's worship and desire for nearness to the Lord brought the revelation of the sacrificial system of worship and approach to God on Mt. Sinai. In fact, both Moses and Abraham created an atmosphere friendly to the presence of the Almighty through obedient faith and worship.

The Lord draws near to those whom He can trust and makes Himself familiar to the heart that worships and acquaints His ways with a life ready to obey.

2. To acquaint yourself with God means to be in harmony with Him.

This means I agree with God's assessment of my life—and everything else. I don't argue with the promptings of His Spirit which may be contrary to my inclinations. Instead, I yield to Him and don't disregard the Word. I submit to its authority and obey its instruction. I do not neglect the *Word* of God because my desire is to do the *will* of God. Amos 3:3 asks, *"Do two walk together unless they have agreed to do so?"* The Lord walks with and makes Himself known to those who come into agreement with Him.

3. To acquaint yourself with God means to be of service to Him.

It is a matter of becoming "user-friendly" to the Lord for the sake of the Gospel. The apostle Paul overcame a strict Jewish heritage and training in order to become serviceable to the Father. It is his life story.

Accompanying signs and wonders in Paul's ministry, and revelations he received from the Lord which occupy the greater majority of the New Testament, testify to the fact that he created an environment friendly to the presence of God.

4. To acquaint yourself with God means to minister to Him.

We minister to the Lord in our expressions of worship and praise. In so doing we create a lifestyle which welcomes and ushers in His presence.

Praise involves what is communicated from our mouths and consistent with our actions. *"Let us continually offer the sacrifice of praise to God, that is, the fruit of our lips, giving thanks to His name"* (Hebrews 13:15 NKJV). Praise also makes way for God's presence. *"You are holy, enthroned in the praises of Israel"* (Psalm 22:3 NKJV).

_____ ⌐*₩₩₩⌐⌐ _____

The power of our praise should never be underestimated. We drive back the unseen powers of darkness and purge spiritual atmospheres with genuine expression of adoration toward the Lord.

David's praise brought a climate conducive to the presence of the Lord, and in so doing created an atmosphere hostile to the demonic presence that troubled king Saul (1 Samuel 16:23). Furthermore, his psalms and worship and his successes in battle were inter-related. He was victorious on the battlefield because His praise invited the presence of the Lord.

This was David's own testimony: *"With Your help I can advance against a troop; with my God I can scale a wall...It is God who arms me with strength and makes my way perfect...He trains my hands for battle"* (2 Samuel 22:30,33,35).

_____ ⌐*₩₩₩⌐⌐ _____

We acquaint ourselves with the Lord when we minister to Him in praise and worship.

We must produce an atmosphere in our lives, homes, jobs and in our churches which is friendly to Jehovah's presence.

THE CONDITIONAL PROMISE OF HIS PRESENCE

Jesus promised, *"Again, I tell you that if two of you on earth agree about anything you ask for, it will be done for you by My Father in heaven. For where two or three come together in My name, there am I with them"* (Matthew 18:19-20). The word *"For"* ties Matthew 18:20 to the previous verse which makes agreeing together the condition for the presence of Christ's Spirit.

A brief word study of Matthew 18:20 gives us a better

understanding of the glorious prospects of such a promise. *"Where two or three are gathered..."* *"Gathered"* (sunago/Greek) is a two-part word "sun" and "ago." "Sun" means "union association, companionship, resemblance." "Ago" in the original is "to induce, to bring, to lead." *"In My name..."* *"In"* in the Greek (eis) translates, "the point entered or the place reached; the time or purpose."

"My Name" speaks of the title of Jesus being representative of His person, power, purpose, promises and praiseworthiness. *"There I am in their midst."* *"In"* (en/Greek) refers to "a fixed position (place, time, state) implying for the purpose of intermediation or constructive instrumentality." *"In their midst"* is the equivalent to the "Shechinah" or special presence of God visible in the wilderness tabernacle (Exodus 40:34) and the temple of Solomon (2 Chronicles 5:14).

The promise Jesus is making in Matthew 18:20 is spiritually exhilarating when we take a moment and consider it in its fullness.

- *"Wherever two or three are gathered"*—Induced, lead and brought together in companionship and similitude and in union with Me and one another, at a specific place and time.
- *"In My name"*—For the purpose of declaring the praiseworthiness of My name. For the objective of confessing their need for what the power of My name can provide. For the purpose of laying claims to the promises I have made which "My name" stands behind.
- *"There"*—In that place, state and point in time, I will be present as the intermediatory instrument (Savior) for their needed redemption, and as the constructive instrument (Creator) for their needed miracle. I will be present every time and in every place where these conditions and purposes characterize the gathering.
- *"I am present in their midst"*— Although unseen, yet My presence is as equivalent to and as real and valid as My "schechinah," or special presence which was visible in the tabernacle of the wilderness and Solomon's temple in Jerusalem.

THE CONDITIONS

The promised presence of Jesus in the local church is predicated upon meeting two requirements.

First, it is conditional on being a people whose hearts and minds are in agreement. This means they are a church which rightly discerns the body of Christ (1 Corinthians 11:29) in their relationships toward one another as well as toward Jesus' gift of pastoral leadership (Ephesians 4:11-13).

It is a church were fellowship with one another springs from their individual and personal relationship with Jesus and involves unconditional love and acceptance that does not exploit or manipulate one another. It is also a "spiritual community" where there is "supernatural togetherness" and Holy Spirit directed movement and growth toward a complete fullness in Christ.

This does not mean they just ask for the same things in prayer. Rather, it indicates there is agreement which is empowered by the fact they have obediently endeavored to *"keep the unity of the Spirit in the bond of peace"* (Ephesians 4:3 NKJV) and are in right relationship with one another and with the Lord.

Second, it is conditional upon embracing the God-given vision and being committed to the mission the Lord has given to them for their city through pastoral leadership. They set aside their personal agendas to see the greater one accomplished and are willing to give sacrificially of time, money and prayer to see the mission accomplished.

They are willing to take steps together in what they know to be the will of God as a vision communicated by His anointed and appointed leadership. Even more, they really believe that as they do this together, *"He is able to do exceedingly abundantly above all that we ask or think according to the power that works in us"* (Ephesians 3:20 NKJV).

THE UNFORTUNATE REALITY FOR TOO MANY CHURCHES

Sadly, division and strife within a congregation always hinders, quenches and resists the presence of God's Spirit. In contrast, the following illustration is an actual church scenario for which I have first hand knowledge.

A pastor was elected to lead a church which for many decades prior to his coming had struggled under financial bondage which threatened the church's very existence. During his predecessor's pastoral tenure, although there had been steady numerical growth and substantial financial gains had been made, disunity and strife had split the church four times. On each occasion, a disgruntled pastoral staff member left and took a sizeable number of the congregation to begin another church within driving distance in the same city.

Much to his own disadvantage and blame for not knowing, the new pastor gained knowledge of this history only after arriving on the scene. Needless to say, the few years that ensued under the newly-elected pastor's ministry was an experience the likes of which he never imagined. The war of words over music "styles" in worship was raging when he arrived. And even though "contemporary" and "traditional" worship services were offered, and the music director he hired was a talented, professional musician and vocal arranger as well as an anointed worship leader who pursued the "middle of the road" in music style, very little peace and harmony could be found.

One regular attendee who had been in the church for a number of years, standing in close proximity to the sound booth during a Sunday morning pre-service practice and sound check expressed his disapproval by actually challenging the music pastor physically if changes to his liking were not made.

One of the musicians for the worship band, in an angry response over what he perceived to be the music pastor's insensitive requirement over not having music learned on the eve of an Easter production, stormed out of rehearsal and into the senior pastor's office slamming his fist into the palm of his hand saying, "Who the _ _ _ _ does he think he is?!"

He then retaliated by threatening to quit, bailing out of the production at the last minute.

The vision and mission the Lord had given the pastoral leadership for the church in reaching their community was undermined by criticism and open opposition toward other pastoral staff members the senior pastor had hired. Another departmental ministry program leader and long-time Christian expressed concern to another associate pastor over the "kind" of people who had started attending their church since they had begun new outreaches to a multi-cultural community.

When the weary pastor finally resigned, a long-time member of the same church spoke openly of having withheld his tithe support in protest of the leadership and the direction of the church during this time. And after the pastor left, an associate and "friend" of the senior minister who had obviously sided with the critics, began campaigning and making it known to those in authority of his desire to be considered as the interim, if not possibly the next senior pastor.

GRACE AND PEACE: THE MARKS OF CHRIST'S PRESENCE

It is possible to have church without the presence of the Lord. But it is impossible to experience "grace and peace" which is needed in these final days without the presence of the Lord. It is from this perspective of Christ standing in the midst of the seven lampstands (the church) that John pronounces this blessing of *"grace and peace to you from Him who is and who was and who is to come, from the seven Spirits who are before His throne, and from Jesus Christ..."* (Revelation 1:4).

The grace and peace of Christ are not commodities
or qualities of life we receive apart from His presence
—which brings these valuable attributes.

Grace is the undeserved gift of His favor and enabling. Peace is the calm assurance of mind and heart the Holy Spirit gives to those who put their trust completely in Jesus Christ.

When God's people cherish and guard the *"unity of Spirit in the bonds of peace"* then the Lord's presence is a reality. You can tangibly feel it when you walk into churches. Some call it the church's personality, while others refer to it as attitude. But, in reality, it is the wonderful presence of the Lord you can sense, and the stimulus to worship God in humble reverence or the liberty of joyous celebration which is unmistakably present.

Although generational and cultural differences make certain music styles a matter of personal preference among God's people, this ceases to be a divisive issue where congregations have met the conditions for the Spirit of Christ to be present in their worship gathering.

GRACE AND PEACE

In the Book of Revelation we view the scenes of God's declared judgment coming on nations and His wrath outpoured upon an unbelieving humanity, which have been kept back since Christ's atoning death at Calvary. But in the church which Jesus shepherds there will be grace. For there is also an innumerable multitude who have washed their robes in the blood of the Lamb (Revelation 7:9-14).

It is said of the early church that *"great grace was upon them all"* (Acts 4:33 NKJV). And so it shall be true of this last days church which Jesus pastors.

In Revelation, God declares there shall be war and bloodshed, carnage and conflict, the crash of empires, anarchy, oppression, despair and terror, war in the heavenlies and war in the earth, an incarnated beast indwelt and driven by Satan himself, stars falling from heaven, plagues and demons greatly influencing human affairs. However, in the church Jesus is shepherding there will be peace.

In the midst of great challenge and opposition, it is said of the early church that *"throughout Judea, Galilee and Samaria the churches had peace and were edified. And walking in the fear of the Lord and the comfort of the Holy Spirit they were multiplied"* (Acts 9:31 NKJV).

201

And so it shall be in this "last days" church.

John declares, *"grace to you and peace from Him."* And more than any and all manifestation and demonstrations of the Holy Spirit's working in the church which may and shall be experienced, this is the promised reality of His presence: *"grace and peace from Him."*

THE STIMULUS FOR TRUE WORSHIP

When we understand it is possible to realize His presence in our midst, to have Him present as Savior and miracle worker, the dispenser of peace and the giver of grace, this becomes the great stimulus and inspiration for worship and praise in our lives and in the church.

In corporate gatherings it is no longer just a musical concert containing a creative blend of my favorite "style" of music. Never forget that music is God's gift to us, not our gift to God. What we present to the Lord is worship and praise.

As much of a Spirit-inspired creation our church music might be, the songs serve only as the vehicle by which hearts and lives "in agreement" petition His presence to be near and invite Him to minister as He has determined to do so in any particular gathering. God doesn't listen to the music anyway! This may surprise us and insult our pride, yet the fact is, all He listens to is what the Holy Spirit is singing from within the hearts of true worshipers.

In the church Jesus is shepherding, corporate praise and worship becomes our quest for His manifest presence. Even more, the realization of His nearness becomes the stimulus for true worship.

CHAPTER THIRTEEN

A RELEASE OF THE RESURRECTION POWER OF JESUS TO ADVANCE THE KINGDOM OF CHRIST

*"Jesus Christ the faithful witness, the firstborn from the dead...
who loved us and washed us from our sins in His own blood and
has made us kings and priests to His God and Father...I am He
who lives and was dead, and behold I am alive forevermore,
Amen. And I have the keys of Hell and death."*
– REVELATION 1:5,6,18 NKJV

In my opinion, the late Keith Greene was to the "Jesus Movement" in the 70s what Bob Dylan was to the "Hippie Movement." In some ways they were both the unofficial "poet laureates" of their constituency.

Keith Greene's music joyously celebrated the life we have in Christ, and at the same time it thundered with prophetic anointing calling a generation to live righteously and surrender to Christ's Lordship. His own lyrics best described his brand of discipleship in one song saying, "I pledge my head to heaven." In another, he wrote an indictment against spiritual lukewarmness with the accompanying loss of passion and power in Christian living with his admonishment,

"Jesus rose from the dead and you can't even get out of bed!"

THE MINISTRY OF KINGS AND PRIESTS

John declares in the opening chapter of the Book of Revelation that through the resurrection, Christ's power over death and Hell has won the most colossal victory in all of the universe for all the ages. And it has brought the release of Christ's resurrection power to those who have, by repentance and faith, become eligible recipients of it.

His resurrection has empowered us to become "kings and priests" to God. As "kings," Christ has delegated to us His spiritual authority to confront and overrule the "works of the devil" in this world. *"For this purpose the Son of God was manifested, that He might destroy (render powerless) the works of the devil"* (1 John 3:8 NKJV).

He has given to us this authority of His which has rendered powerless the works of the devil. Jesus said, *"And as you go, preach, saying, 'The kingdom of heaven is at hand.' Heal the sick, cleanse the lepers, raise the dead, cast out demons. Freely you have received, freely give"* (Matthew 10:7-8 NKJV).

Through prayer, righteous living, obedient faith and the proclamation of the Gospel of Jesus there is released the power of the Almighty to advance the Kingdom of Christ in the hearts and lives of men and women. As "priests" unto God we have been delegated spiritual authority and privilege to minister healing and deliverance and to enforce the will of the Lord through prayerful intercession.

Priestly ministry is the call and anointing to stand before God on behalf of people. This call includes meeting practical human needs and to alleviate human suffering as well. Jesus told us how this is accomplished. *"...for I was hungry and you gave Me food; I was thirsty and you gave Me drink; I was a stranger and you took Me in; I was naked and you clothed Me; I was sick and you visited Me; I was in prison and you came to Me...Assuredly, I say to you, inasmuch as you did it to one of the least of these My brethren, you did it to Me"* (Matthew 25:35-36,40 NKJV).

James included caring for widows and orphans as the test of acceptable religious profession. *"Religion that God our Father accepts as pure and faultless is this: to look after orphans and widows in their distress and to keep oneself from being polluted by the world"* (James 1:26-27).

How many times have we read these portions of Scripture and acknowledged the power of the Gospel to change lives but failed to share the Gospel with those in our sphere of influence? How often have we been appreciative of private social services and government agencies for the caring work they do in behalf of the needy and hurting, yet we never include any such ministry programming or staffing in the church's budget?

Jesus said, *"But you shall receive power when the Holy Spirit has come upon you; and you shall be witnesses to Me in Jerusalem, and in all Judea and Samaria, and to the end of the earth"* (Acts 1:8 NKJV).

Pentecostal power wasn't needed in the upper room of Acts 2:4. It was, however, needed in the streets of Jerusalem to confirm the witness of the Gospel with signs and wonders which included changed lives, healings and deliverance. And it was imperative to move the believers into compassionate need-meeting ministry to a hurting world.

―――――――

A release of the resurrection power of Jesus to advance the Kingdom of Christ accompanies this kind of wholistic vision and mission.

THE POTENTIAL OF THE CHURCH

Bayside Church (Covenant affiliation) of Granite Bay, California, is one of these churches. It started in 1995 with just a few praying people. Under the leadership of pastor Ray Johnston it has grown to a congregation of over eight thousand. Because they were only allowed by the city to build a 2,000-seat auditorium, they have included an aggressive church-planting program as part of their vision. As I write these words, this congregation has already planted three vibrant and growing churches in the greater Sacramento area with a vision for planting many more.

At their tenth year anniversary (April, 2005), they launched the vision for their next chapter of ministry as a historical opportunity to join together in growing in Christ, reaching out to their community, and demonstrating compassion around the world. In addition, this $12.5 million vision and mission included the following:

Planting Churches
- Plant 15-20 new churches in the Sacramento, CA, region in the next 3-5 years.
- Help the church in Indonesia by planting 2 churches through "Partners International."
- Plant a thriving church in Iraq through "Frontiers."
- Plant a church in an unreached area of India through "Seed Group" that will be pivotal in community transformation
- Plant 2 churches in Cambodia with "Reaksha."

Assisting the Poor
- Assist in starting a local women and family center to help them get off the streets and become emotionally, physically and spiritually healthy.
- Provide wheelchairs for disabled children and adults in four countries through the Joni and Friends program, "Wheels for the World."
- Support orphanages that are transforming the lives of children who have been left alone because of the AIDS crises, or who have been neglected and abandoned on the streets.
- Transformation training in Kenya through "Empowering Lives."

Caring for the Sick
- Help build and staff a medical center to enhance the ministry of the "Faith Alive Clinic" in Nigeria.
- Partner with a Covenant hospital in the Congo to provide medical supplies, equipment, building upgrade and remodel of the facility.

- Hire a staff person to partner with "Global Strategies" to help reduce the AIDS crisis.

EDUCATING THE NEXT GENERATION
- Do extreme facility remodels and material upgrades to provide a proper learning environment for local disadvantaged public schools in Sacramento, CA.

This is the demonstration of resurrection power which can be released to advance the Kingdom of Christ through the vision and ministry of one church. Granted, not every ministry has access to resources like Bayside. But every church is strategically located in its community to accomplish such a vision and mission.

"RADICALLY OBEDIENT FAITH"
God gives of Himself to the local leadership in order for a church to realize its destiny. The tragic history of so many congregations is that as the neighborhood changes around them, they sell the buildings and move rather than retain a vibrant ministry to their community. Relocating to an area which is more "desirable" is the option preferred rather than addressing the challenges of a changing demographic through prayer, vision-casting and strategic ministry planning. When they do so, the congregation ceases to be "kings and priests" unto God with a release of resurrection power to advance Christ's kingdom in that community.

We must never forget we are not just recipients of resurrection life. We are channels through which it flows in healing and redemptive power to others.

Nothing short of radically obedient faith and supremely prioritizing the task of evangelism will bring such a release of resurrection power in and through the church. We can pray for more power, but the Lord sees the heart of the church and He knows whether or not we are willing to utilize this power for the sake of touching a hurting and dying world with the Gospel.

The Spirit of God knows whether we desire biblical "spiritual manifestations" for the sake of validating our "spiritual posture" or for fulfilling His missionary commission to reach our world. To the church that left Him outside knocking at the front door, Jesus said, *"I know your deeds, that you are neither cold nor hot. I wish you were either one or the other! So, because you are lukewarm—neither hot nor cold—I am about to spit you out of My mouth. You say, 'I am rich; I have acquired wealth and do not need a thing.' But you do not realize that you are wretched, pitiful, poor, blind and naked"* (Revelation 3:15-17).

Jesus didn't say He *"saw* their deeds," rather, He *"knew* their deeds." Man sees our actions, but God knows what's behind them. And Jesus knew that the deeds of the Laodicean church were really the expression of a heart which was lukewarm toward Him and the calling upon their life and ministry.

What good would it do for a church such as this to ask for more power when they had no passion?

Ironically it's as if Jesus was saying if you don't reach out passionately to the "wretched, pitiful, poor, blind and naked" with My love and the message of the Gospel, in reality that's what you become in so far as your relationship with Me.

THE RESURRECTION POWER

Jesus boldly declared, *"The Spirit of the Lord is on Me, because He has anointed Me to preach good news to the poor. He has sent Me to proclaim freedom for the prisoners and recovery of sight for the blind, to release the oppressed, to proclaim the year of the Lord's favor"* (Luke 4:18-19).

Resurrection power is released to advance Christ's Kingdom in the church that accepts Jesus' assignment and anointing for ministry as their own. This power is given for spiritual authority as "kings and priests" unto God to minister supernaturally as well as practically to the needs of people in Jesus' name. This power is Christ's provision of the Holy Spirit's influence in and through the church which confronts the life-quenching power of Hell at every level of human living, and defeats it by introducing the power of the Gospel to impart the miracle of life in the Spirit through new birth.

All Christ has accomplished in His death and resurrection is to become a life and ministry reality. In the church that Jesus shepherds, this release of His power is advancing His Kingdom on earth.

WHY THE CHURCH HAS NOT YET REACHED THIS WORLD WITH THE GOSPEL

Jesus said, *"And this Gospel of the kingdom will be preached in all the world as a witness to the all the nations, and then the end will come"* (Matthew 24:14 NKJV).

Why have over 2000 years gone by and this has not yet been accomplished? I offer at least three scriptural reasons as to why this is the case:

1. Reaching the world with the Gospel requires a soul-winning lifestyle.

The ministry of soul-winning is not a religious professional career, rather a lifestyle centered in relationship with Jesus Christ.

In every church we hear dear people apologize because they are shy and introverted in personality and therefore cannot witness. But we have the mistaken idea you need to be a gifted communicator to share the Gospel with others.

My professor in seminary told our Greek language class a story one day which illustrates how the Lord can use anyone who has been moved to compassion to share the truth about eternity and the decision that everyone needs to make concerning the claims of Jesus.

A very simple and introverted young man was moved powerfully by a challenge at church to reach the lost. What especially struck him was the fact that without Christ even his friends and family would spend eternity in Hell. He had a neighbor who always spoke in a kind and friendly manner toward him, and as a result of the soul-winning challenge he became concerned for his soul.

One day the man summoned enough nerve to speak with his friend concerning his spiritual condition. In his own clumsy, stuttering way he asked the man, "Are you going to heaven?"

The surprised neighbor looked at him for a moment that seemed like eternity to the young man. And still staring at him he answered, "I don't know!"

This shy Christian was so unnerved by the conversation which he had initiated, he immediately forgot all his soul-winning training and, completely flustered, didn't quite know how to end the conversation. So in his frustration and embarrassment he blurted out, "Well go to Hell then!" and walked away.

He became so mortified at what he had said that he didn't know if he could *ever* face his neighbor again. But Jesus knew the heart of the young man and what had motivated him.

Believe it or not, this was exactly what God knew was needed to capture the neighbor's attention.

The Holy Spirit brought an unrest to the man's heart and mind he could not shake.

He was confronted as he had never been before to consider the reality of heaven and Hell and the eternal implications for his own soul in that one simple question.

Before long the neighbor found his way to the young man's church, gave his life to Christ and shared his testimony there as to what had happened.

If nothing else this story serves as a reminder of what Paul said. *"But this precious treasure—this light and power that now shine within us—is held in a perishable container, that is, in our weak bodies. Everyone can see that the glorious power within must be from God and is not our own"* (2 Corinthians 4:7 NLT).

In Acts chapter one Jesus gave His followers one clear statement which supercedes all other even legitimate ministry concerns. He told them the "times and seasons" of eschatology were the Father's business, but soul-winning was always in season. It was always time to share the Gospel with people. And that's what He commanded them to do. In fact, the power of the Holy Spirit would be poured out upon them first and foremost for this very work. *"But you will receive power when the Holy Spirit comes on you; and you will be My witnesses in Jerusalem, and in all Judea and Samaria, and to the ends of the earth"* (Acts 1:8).

As the believers gave themselves to *"being witnesses to Him"* (this means telling others what they had personally experienced concerning faith in Jesus), within ten years Jerusalem was rocked to its foundations. And the cities around the Mediterranean basin from Jerusalem to Rome were stirred and thousands came to personal faith in the Lord Jesus Christ.

Every new Christian became a witness for Christ, and together with a few evangelists gifted and called to present the Gospel in clarity and power, they worked hand in hand in the church's task of making disciples among all nations.

Certainly there were crowds who heard the Gospel, but the personal call is first for each one to *reach* one. It is the story presented to us in the Gospels of Andrew finding Peter, Philip finding Nathaniel and each bringing them to Jesus.

The directive of Christ in Matthew chapter ten tells us that a personal soul-winning lifestyle involves several things:

First, it involves contact.
"Go to the lost sheep of Israel" (Matthew 10:6).
Jesus sent people to personally contact those within their sphere of influence. It was first to be personal and out of relationship with others. This is what makes us a credible witness.

Second, it involves communication.
As you go, preach saying, *'The Kingdom of Heaven is at hand"* (Matthew 10:7 NKJV).
There must be relevant communication of the Gospel to the culture in the language of the culture. People will die and go to Hell

wondering what made the difference in our lives if we don't communicate what caused our transformation.

Third, it involves human compassion and supernatural power.

"Heal the sick, cleanse the leper, raise the dead, cast out demons. Freely you've received, freely give" (Matthew 10:8 NKJV).

There is no other demonstration of the love and compassion of Christ to this world other than through the lives of His followers. Jesus said it was by our love for one another the world would know we were His disciples (John 13:35).

We give freely because we have received freely. God's people are givers not takers because that's who God is. People sense real love because it is the most humanly convincing argument for the validity of the Gospel. It is our compassion which opens the heart's door to the message of Christ. And it is the Holy Spirit who walks through that door and makes the supernatural change in their lives. Both the human and divine are intertwined together.

Fourth, it involves consistent and persistent effort.

"Whatever city or town you enter...stay there til you go out..." (Matthew 10:11 NKJV).

In a feel-good culture we want a convenient Christianity. However, soul-winning is an energetic commitment to the commission of Jesus Christ to His church, not an obligatory connection to a program of the ministry. We can love our church and not love the lost—and love the ministry and not love a dying world.

We can do our "church thing" and never do Christ's "Kingdom thing." But we can't love Jesus and not be moved to share His amazing love with others! It is a commitment of love which is both consistent and persistent.

Fifth, it involves conflict.

"And whoever will not receive you nor hear your words, when you depart from that house or city, shake off the dust from your feet" (Matthew 10:14 NKJV).

Oh, what fragile egos we nurse! One of the unhappy secrets of the

212

Christian life is that Jesus hasn't cried all the tears or been on the receiving end of all the rejection. There's still some of this left for us to deal with.

One of the most graphic examples I ever experienced was when a friend and I were handing out tracks and witnessing in the downtown area of one of our major west coast cities. A man walked up to us, looked at my friend and spat in his face. As the spittle was literally dripping off the end of my friend's nose, the man's enraged countenance made him believable when he said, "If I had a gun, right now I'd shoot you dead!"

Conflict is inevitable:

- When the message of righteousness confronts unrighteousness.
- When light confronts darkness.
- When salt confronts putrification and decay.
- When love confronts bigotry and hatred.
- When truth confronts error.
- When honesty confronts deception.
- When God's Word confronts philosophy and opinion.
- When the Spirit of Christ living in you confronts the *"spirit who is now at work in those who are disobedient"* (Ephesians 2:2).

With regards to this conflict the Gospel would engender, Jesus tells us, *"Don't imagine that I came to bring peace to the earth! No, rather, a sword. I have come to set a man against his father, and a daughter against her mother, and a daughter-in-law against her mother-in-law—a man's worst enemies will be right in his own home! If you love your father and mother more than you love Me, you are not worthy of being Mine; or if you love your son or daughter more than Me, you are not worthy of being Mine. If you refuse to take up your cross and follow Me, you are not worthy of being Mine"* (Matthew 10:34-38 TLB).

It is a lifestyle in which privacy concerning personal faith in Christ is not a right! Because of what we have received from Jesus, we are debtors to humanity at all times in all places. When we stand before the Lord to receive our reward, if not for winning souls to Christ what else can we legitimately and scripturally expect Him to reward us for?

Paul said of those who had come to Christ through his ministry, *"For what is our hope, our joy, or the crown in which we will glory in the presence of our Lord Jesus when He comes? Is it not you? Indeed, you are our glory and joy"* (1 Thessalonians 2:19-20).

- People are spiritually blind and we must lead them to Jesus, the Sight Giver.
- People are bound and we must bring them to Jesus, the Deliverer.
- People are "spiritually terminal" and we must bring them to Jesus, the Healer.
- People are spiritually dead and we must bring them to the One who halts funeral processions, calls them by name and commands them to "Come forth!"

2. Reaching the world with the Gospel requires unity in the church.

Of all the devil's warfare strategies against the church's effectiveness in fulfilling the Great Commission of Christ, breeding disunity has always been—and still is—the most lethal. Why else is it that one of the greatest "hot buttons" for disagreement and strife in the church arises when a new, creative or revolutionary outreach program which endangers some "sacred cows" and means spending money is introduced?

How many churches do you know who have spent themselves poor in outreach programming and ministry to the lost? Compare this to how many churches you may know who are in grave financial situations because they built multi-million dollar facilities but they are not passionately and tenaciously committed to filling it with new converts from their community?

Why should the Lord help to finance a perpetually vacant building? Why should you or I?

Everything God is and has been doing in human affairs and in the nations of the world since the Fall is centered in redemption. In his book "Destined for the Throne," Paul E. Billheimer states the universe was created for one purpose and that was to provide a suitable habitation for the human race.

We were created in the image and likeness of God to provide an eternal companion for the Father and become a bride for the Son of God.

The nation of Israel was chosen for one purpose: to bring to this world the birth of the Messiah. He came for one intent: to give birth to the church through redemption by His atoning death and resurrection. The church (mankind redeemed through personal faith in Jesus Christ) is the central object and goal of history and what God has been doing in all realms from all eternity.

Every event in history transpires to serve one purpose; the proclamation of the Gospel of Jesus Christ, which is *"the power of God at work, saving everyone who believes"* (Romans 1:16 NLT).

The church as the dwelling place of Christ's Spirit is the instrument of God's redemptive purpose. As the church goes, so goes the world!

In his book "Sodom Had No Bible," Lenoard Ravenhill itemizes Satan's agenda which stands in opposition to the soul-winning ministry of the body of Christ. He states a Satanic objective is in place to keep living men and women eating, drinking and partying through life oblivious to the reality that without Christ they are only one heartbeat away from an inconceivably horrible Hell.

- It is to keep living men and women captive in chains of fear, lust, anger, greed, rebellion and hatred—then after this life is over, hold them eternal prisoners in the bottomless pit.
- It is to squander resources of talent, time and finance on things which end when life does.
- It is to trample the sacrifice of Christ's precious blood under foot and scorn it as filth.

- It is to cheat Jesus, the eternal King of Life and Glory, of the love which He so royally deserves from men and women who could be born again by the miracle power of the Holy Spirit.

The way Satan often accomplishes this is by causing disunity, strife and division in the church.

In His book "Evangelism by Fire," evangelist Reinhardt Bohnke uses the account in Judges 4 and 5 to give scriptural insight into the division and misplaced priorities which hamper unified evangelism efforts in the church. These two chapters record a battle which takes place simultaneously both on earth and in the spirit realm.

The response of the tribes of Israel who were called to enter that battle illustrates how effective evangelism and missions is a unified, corporate call to spiritual warfare.

The prophetess Deborah was called by the Lord to deliver Israel from Canaanite plundering and killing which was occurring at the time. In this act of deliverance of Israel, God chose to use Deborah through her persuasive powers of speech and her prophetic inspiration. Her call was to rally the men of the nation to warfare under the leadership of Barak.

In Judges 4 she sent letters by messengers to every tribe in Israel enlisting them to unite and stand in battle. In the next chapter Deborah reflects on the victorious battle and analyzes the response of the tribes to the call to warfare. Viewing the reaction of the various tribes to the prophetic challenge put forth is illustrative of the church's response to the Great Commission of Christ today.

The tribe of Reuben's response could earn them the label of "philosophical spiritualizers" or "critical analysts."
"Among the divisions of Reuben there were great resolves of heart ...the divisions of Reuben have great searchings of heart" (Judges 5:15-16 NKJV). They aimed well but never pulled the trigger. They prayerfully and thoughtfully considered the urgent request of Deborah, yet didn't believe they should rush off to battle without a masterful plan.

The tribe of Reuben were the thinkers and planners, the philosophizers and spiritualizers of logistical procedure. They would be glad to pray for Deborah and those involved in the fierce fighting, but they just couldn't, with clear reason, be responsible for giving their full approval of the way things were being done.

These people found something disagreeable about the methods, the leadership, the timing, the personnel, the weaponry, the "whatever." They hid behind an analytical, philosophical smokescreen of inactivity, having "great searchings of heart."

In the end, however, they listed their objections and questioned as to why they should give themselves wholeheartedly in unity with others for the rescue of souls.

The admonition we should take from the tribe of Reuben is to major on the "majors" and minor on the "minors." The insignificant minutia must never outweigh the major concerns.

There is just one vital matter on the heart of Jesus
—and it should be on the mind and heart of the church.
What is this concern? To wage war against Satan
in the spiritual campaign for souls.

Giving our thoughts to critical analysis and philosophical spiritualizing and justifying our church quarrels when *"hell has enlarged herself and opened her mouth without measure"* (Isaiah 5:14 KJV) is a trivial pursuit which is beyond profane. It is minutely comparable to Congress debating over the best camouflage color and uniform designs for law enforcement and military while terrorist bombs are exploding in our cities.

While the Great Commission from Jesus to His church resembles a military draft call up—not a suggestion for consideration—the Reubenites have only "great searchings of heart."

The tribe of Asher could be called the "balanced life seekers."
"Asher continued at the seashore and stayed by his inlets" (Judges 5:17 NKJV).

217

This man worked hard at his job. Church duties were okay for those whose lives and livelihoods were not quite as significant as his. Asherites have lifestyle interests to pursue and the need to be balanced with their involvement in the church's soul-winning warfare.

Right now this "balanced life" calls for time off from church work. They applaud the commitments of others and even pray and believe for victory, but they also depend on others to do what would call them beyond the balanced life. It always seems to get done without them anyway!

Asher is one reason the church is run by tired people. Someone coined a humorous adage which says "Statistically 20% are the pillars of the church while 80% are the caterpillars that crawl in and out every week!"

Jesus' parable of the workers in the vineyard points out how all the workers were paid the same by the landowner because each had worked as long as they had the chance to work. Ten years out of eighty, alive and working for Jesus in the harvest of souls, is better than any consistently lukewarm life ever lived no matter how long. These extraordinary times call for extraordinary people!

While the great battle of the ages is waging for the souls of mankind, and while the army could be greatly strengthened by reinforcements and the tide of the battle could be turned for tens of thousands, *"Asher* (the balanced life seeker) *continued by the seashore."*

The tribe of Dan struggled with misplaced priorities and conflicts of personal interest.

Deborah asked, *"Why did Dan remain on ships?"* (Judges 5:17 NKJV).

The Danites were ship merchants, dealing in the supply of material goods to Israel. Their vessels, moored in the harbors, became retail shops.

When the call came from Deborah to make the battle a priority, profits were at an all-time high and their many interests just wouldn't allow them to cut out another slice from the commitment pie. Besides, how customers might feel about such a personal dedication to radical soul-winning methods in the community might become a public relations problem as well.

Dan had been willing to take daring risks for the sake of building his business, but he wasn't ready to "trust it all" in the hands of God who now called him to prioritize the Kingdom business of souls.

The Danites are those who hear the call of God upon their lives. But misplaced priorities create such a conflict when it comes to time and interest taken to respond to this call, they lose the vision for what their life could mean for Christ—and for impacting their hurting and dying generation with the Gospel.

American poet Whittier says it so well.
"Of all the words of tongue or pen, the saddest are
these; 'What might have been.'"

When soul-winning is not a priority, the church can actually maintain multimillion dollar facilities which accommodate spiritually dry gatherings in order to pacify bored parishioners who constantly remind the leadership they're the ones who have bought and paid for it all. And all the while the world around them hits the trail for Hell at a speed which is off the radar screen.

The tribes of Zebulun and Naphtali were the soul-winning warriors.

"Zebulun is a people who jeopardized their lives to the point of death. Napthali also, on the heights of the battlefield" (Judges 5:18 NKJV).

The people of these tribes weren't any different from others who were also looking forward to the end of a work week and the joy of family time. But when the call to war came from the prophetess Deborah, there was only one response from them. It was, "Let's go! And praise the Lord that God has anointed somebody to hear from heaven and lead us.

It's about time we started winning this battle!" Engaging the struggle for souls was not just something they did, it was the

219

expression of who they were.

The battle was won, yet victory came without Dan, Reuben and Asher. And we will be triumphant today as well. But at what cost of human souls and for how long?

So far it's only taken two thousand years! How long before we begin winning the battle in our neighborhood, city, nation and our world? What are we willing to do to come together and fulfill the Great commission of Christ to His church? This requires unity.

3. The church has not yet reached the world with the Gospel because we fail to remember that human souls are the only inheritance Jesus has.

Soul winning is infinitely more than a church growth or a transformation of society issue. Jesus has placed His glory and eternal inheritance in the hands of the church's evangelism endeavor. It is the honor of Jesus which is at stake. *"I will declare the decree: The LORD has said to Me, 'You are My Son, Today I have begotten You. Ask of Me, and I will give You the nations for Your inheritance, And the ends of the earth for Your possession'"* (Psalm 2:7-8 NKJV).

When God the Father promised Christ His Son the nations as His inheritance it refers to the *redeemed* from every nation (Revelation 5:9-10). These are Christ's inheritance.

The word "inheritance" in Hebrew (nachala) is "a possession to which one has received legal claim by rights of family." Only the redeemed are the born again members of the family of God.

Each of the tribes of Israel received a portion of the Promised Land and it was determined by casting lots (Numbers 26:56) and then apportioned to them by Joshua after the death of Moses (Joshua 11:23).

The land was each family's inheritance, a possession which was the result of the conquest of Canaan. It could not be given away or sold to anyone outside of the family.

YOUR INHERITANCE
Psalm 2:7-8 is a Messianic psalm depicting the incarnation of

Christ and the stated purpose for the Son of God becoming flesh. This purpose was to make legal claims to an inheritance Christ, too, would win by a conquest He would enter.

God the Father invites Him to make His request. And in John 17:20 Jesus asks for His inheritance in His final prayer before His conquest at the Cross. Jesus said, *"My prayer is not for them alone, I pray also for those who will believe in Me through their message."*

Jesus already had claims to all of creation by rights of being the "Creator." *"All things were made by Him, and without Him was not anything made that was made"* (John 1:3 NKJV). *"For by Him all things were created; things in heaven and on earth, visible and invisible...all things were created by Him and for Him. He is before all things and in Him all things hold together"* (Colossians 1:16-17).

All of the created realm is His. It is *for* Him and held together by His authoritative Word. God has claims to all of it by rights as Creator, but Jesus has claims to His inheritance only by rights of "family."

The Bible is clear that when we are spiritually born again by faith in Christ's death and resurrection, we are adopted into the family of God. *"...you received the Spirit of sonship, and by Him we cry 'Abba Father'"* (Romans 8:15). *"...God sent His Son, born of a woman under the law, to redeem those under the law, that we might receive the full rights of sons. Because you are sons, God sent the Spirit of His Son into our hearts, the Spirit who calls out 'Abba Father'...and since you are a son, God has made you also an heir"* (Galatians 4:4-7). *"...He predestined us to be adopted as His sons through Jesus Christ, in accordance with His pleasure and will, to the praise of His glorious grace..."* (Ephesians 1:5-6).

God's Word also declares it is on the basis of this adoption by the Holy Spirit alone we are the inheritance of Christ Jesus. *"But you are not in the flesh but in the Spirit if indeed the Spirit of God dwells in you. Now if anyone does not have the Spirit of Christ, he is not His"* (Romans 8:9 NKJV).

———— ✺ ————

*Because of His sinless life of obedience to God the
Father, Jesus was victorious in His conquest at the Cross.
His defeat of death, Hell and the grave also secured
His rights to inheritance in this conquest.*

This inheritance, however, is only by rights of those who by faith in His blood have been born again, adopted by the Holy Spirit into the family of God.

It's All About Souls

Jesus is not impressed with our business successes, our beautiful church buildings, our ministry programs, talents and gifts. The reason being is they are already His by rights as Creator before they were ours. They are, in fact, His gifts to us. But what He prays for in John chapter 17 is what is His only by inheritance.

The Lord's greatest desire is toward us who are His children and for those who would believe on His name through our message. His glory is the taking of the heathen for His inheritance. And He can do this only as a legal possession by rights of family inheritance.

Paul said, *"I am not ashamed of the gospel, because it is the power of God for the salvation of everyone who believes..."* (Romans 1:16). This is resurrection power which accompanies the passionate proclamation of the Gospel of Jesus Christ.

The tragedy of the universe is not only the loss of human life as evidenced by Hell's growing population. The catastrophe of the ages is that the church's soul-winning efforts betray her failure to remember that the Savior and Prince of Life has no other inheritance than the souls of humanity.

When Christ shepherds His church there is a release of His resurrection power for the purposes of securing this inheritance and advancing His Kingdom.

It is my prayer the Lord will become your Shepherd today—and for eternity.

FOR A COMPLETE LIST OF
RESOURCES BYTHE AUTHOR OR TO
SCHEDULE SPEAKING ENGAGEMENTS,
CONTACT:

TERRY KIRSHMAN
7323 SUGARWOOD ROAD NE
CANTON, OH 44721

PHONE (BETHEL TEMPLE)
330-330-454-3058

EMAIL: tkirschman@sbcglobal.net